MW00761101

SECONDS

FREYA BARKER

This book was inspired by the Salvation Series written by Corinne Michaels. It is an original work that is published through The Salvation Society.

Copyright © 2020 Freya Barker

Editing:
Karen Hrdlicka

Proofing:
Joanne Thompson

LETTER TO THE READER

Hey all!

Just a few words from me!

First of all, thank you so much for your interest in SECONDS.
As a big fan of Corinne Michaels writings, I'm thrilled to be part of the Salvation Society world!

When I first put pen to paper I had absolutely no idea what I was doing. What was only supposed to be a one-time thing, turned into a passion I'm far from done with after six years and 38 books.

Writing is therapy for me, and through my stories I hope to share a little of what it has given me: HOPE.

My dream is for my readers to find that same 'hope' in my words. Not just for love and romance, but for a good, happy, satisfying life, regardless of current circumstances. To show through my characters that despite roadblocks thrown in our path—with an open mind—we can learn to see and move beyond our limitations. That we can stand strong in the face of adversity, and sometimes as a result of it.

Believe in yourself—in your worth.

I hope you enjoy my stories, and I hope you're able to take something away from them.
Happy reading!

xox
Freya

CHAPTER ONE

Reagan

"Objection!"

I glance over at the prosecutor's desk where my ex-husband jumps to his feet, red-faced.

"What now, Mr. Tory?" the judge, who appears to be running thin on patience, barks.

"Irrelevant, Your Honor. The victim isn't on trial here."

I duck my head to hide my smile, even as I get to my feet as well. I was waiting for his objection when I started questioning my witness about his connection with the victim. It would appear Neil is finally cluing in to my purpose for calling William Cirillo.

"Ms. Cole? Relevance?"

"Yes, Your Honor. It has been my client's testimony from the start; it was Mrs. Winters' own action at the root of the unfortunate accident that ultimately took her life. A claim dismissed by prosecution, touting Sheila Winters' near saint-like reputation ad nauseam. Since Mr. Tory continues to bring up Mrs. Winters' exemplary character, I'm merely trying to establish a more realistic picture."

According to Sean Davies, this wasn't the first time he'd picked up Sheila at the Red Lion on Godwin Boulevard. The pub is close to the highway and a popular stop for truckers and travelers, right down the road from a couple of economy motels.

That's where they'd been heading, my client and the victim, when he lost control of the wheel, hit the ditch, and his van rolled several times before coming to rest against a tree. Sheila, who hadn't been wearing a seat belt at the time because she was busy going down on my client—by his account—was ejected through the windshield and perished at the scene.

Cirillo is a regular at the Red Lion who had his own experience with the victim, which is what I was asking him about when Neil shouted his objection.

"Mr. Tory," Judge Embury calls his attention. "Ms. Cole makes a valid point. Since you've opened the door to Mrs. Winters' character, defense has a right to walk through." He turns his gaze on me, over the rim of his reading glasses clinging desperately to the tip of his nose. "Ms. Cole, you may continue, but I suggest you get to the point."

I do an internal fist pump before sharply nodding in confirmation.

"Of course, Your Honor."

Ten minutes later, Judge Embury hammers his gavel on his desk to try to restore order to the courtroom, as the victim's husband is hauled off by two burly court bailiffs. A quick glance over to the jury box shows most eyes are on the irate man, yelling and struggling against the firm hold the guards have on him. The moment the heavy oak doors shut behind them, all eyes turn front and center, where William Cirillo sits open-mouthed in the witness box.

"Ms. Cole. Any more for this witness?"

"No, Your Honor."

"Would the prosecution like to cross-examine the witness?"

"Yes," Neil snaps, before quickly adding, "Your Honor."

He glares at me before rounding his desk and walking up to Cirillo.

For the next forty-five minutes, he tries every trick in the book to shake William from his testimony without success. The only thing he accomplishes in his frustration is shine a spotlight on the fact the victim was a part-time hooker, who apparently enjoyed the thrill of giving head while her john was operating a moving vehicle.

He finally gives up—clearly disgusted with the witness and angry with me—and stalks back to his table. What he thought would be an easy conviction and another chance to best me, is not looking so good now.

Judge Embury dismisses the witness before calling a recess until court reconvenes on Monday for closing arguments.

"That was good, right?" Sean asks me when the judge disappears into chambers.

"That was very good," I confirm, grinning at him.

I dive under the table for my accordion folder and start stuffing my files in when I can sense Neil looming over me.

"That's low, even for you," he says in a growl.

I shove my chair back and stand up before turning to him. My eyes are level with his, thanks to the six-inch heels that are killing my feet, but it's worth it; they have the desired effect. Neil has always been sensitive to his height, or rather, lack thereof, and I'm not above using that in my favor. Like now.

"Merely doing my job," I reply calmly.

"You just destroyed a good woman's reputation."

That stills my hands. He's trying to get under my skin and knows me well enough to be effective.

"I'm not the one with a propensity for fairy tales, Neil. I deal in facts."

———

"Don't work too late."

I look up to find Sally standing in front of my desk, her coat on, and her purse slung over her shoulder. Beyond her I notice at some point night has fallen outside while I've been slaving over my closing argument.

"I'm sorry, I didn't realize it was this late." I have a tendency to lose myself in what I'm doing and block out the rest of the world.

"Not to worry," she assures me. "Matt is at a sleepover and I didn't have any plans." Matt is her ten-year-old son and the only man in her life. "Nothing but half a bottle of wine and leftover pizza waiting for me tonight."

I stretch my arms over my head and lean back in my chair to loosen the tension in my muscles.

"God, that sounds good. Go home. I won't be far behind you, I'm almost finished here."

"Want me to come in a little early Monday so you can practice on me?" She indicates the yellow legal pad I've been scribbling on for the past hours.

"No need. I won't have to be in court until ten, so just come in at eight. That should give us enough time."

"Sure thing. Have a good weekend."

"You too."

She slips out the door and I watch her through the large window as she makes her way across the parking lot to her car.

I'm not surprised she stayed. Sally is one of the most loyal people I know. She's been my legal assistant for five years and when I left Thatcher, Cleaver, and Associates six months ago, followed me without question. She simply turned in her resignation right after I handed in mine and asked me where we were going next. For months that meant her showing up at my place at eight in the morning, setting up shop in my dining room, until we finally found this small office.

Technically it was my brother, Jackson, who had found it for me. It's a serious step down from my seventeenth floor office with a view of downtown in Norfolk, but the old real estate office in a nondescript one-story building on the edge of town is all mine. Well, at least for the remainder of my two-year lease.

McGregor Bail Bonds owns the building and occupies the office beside mine. I'd been hesitant at first, but the close proximity has already been mutually profitable. They've bounced a few clients my way and I've handed out their number more than once as well. It's turned out to be a surprisingly symbiotic relationship.

I've only really had contact with Pooja, their office manager, but I know that aside from the owner, they have three bondsmen working there. I've seen a couple of guys go in and out of the office at times, but haven't had the pleasure.

When I no longer can ignore the gnawing in my stomach, I pack up my notes and laptop, and shrug into my coat. Whatever needs to be tweaked I can do at home; not like I have big plans anyway. Flicking off lights, I palm my keys and step outside, locking the door behind me before turning toward the parking lot.

And slam face first into a large solid wall.

The deep grunt and large hand landing on my shoulder kick my instincts into high gear. I immediately take a step back and haul up my knee.

CAL

"Christ, woman," I grumble, barely managing to twist enough to have her solid knee land in my thigh muscle instead of where it was aimed.

But the next moment I'm jabbed in my lower ribs and I take a fast step back, letting go of her shoulder. Looking down, I see her fisted hand—keys poking out from between her fingers—coming at me again, and I quickly grab hold of her wrist. She's clearly had some self-defense training.

"Let go!" she yells, her eyes widening when she finally looks up at me.

Fuck. I'm well aware my appearance won't help this situation, since I haven't trimmed my hair—both on my head and on my face—since I left on a skip a month ago.

"Name's Callum McGregor," I quickly inform her when she opens her mouth again, I presume to scream bloody murder. It snaps shut. I carefully let go of her wrist, holding my hands up in case she decides to swing at me again. "I'm getting some identification out of my pocket."

I realize I have her at a disadvantage—blocked in the small alcove housing the entrance to each of our offices—so I quickly pull my driver's license from my wallet and hand it to her.

Her relief is immediate when she scans my information and hands it back. Then she tilts her head to the side as she takes me in.

"You need a haircut."

I'm not sure whether to laugh or be offended at the random observation of a woman I don't even know. A woman I, admittedly, observed through the window with some interest as she shut down the office earlier. Jackson Cole's baby sister is well put-together, to put it mildly, and watching her isn't exactly a hardship. I'm not quite sure what to make of her directness, but I opt to let go of the chuckle I've been trying to hold. A good call, as it turns out, because her mouth quirks up on one end in a sardonic smirk.

"Sorry," she mumbles, sticking out her hand, which I easily swallow in mine. "That was rude. Blame it on nerves. It's nice to meet you, I'm Reagan Cole."

"Likewise, and I should be the one to apologize; I shouldn't have snuck up on you."

I don't notice I've been hanging onto her hand—which fits quite comfortably, folded in mine—until she pulls it back.

"I wasn't paying attention," she counters. "It's been a long day and I was distracted trying to decide what to feed myself."

As illustration, her stomach emits a loud rumble. Her eyes widen as she slaps both hands against her midsection.

I stifle the urge to invite her to Joe's, where I'd intended to go for Mexican after dropping off my files. It's all I could think of these past few days on the road, and sharing a meal with a beautiful woman would be a bonus, but Reagan isn't just any woman. She's Jackson's kid sister, and I seem to recall there being a rule about not lusting after a buddy's sister. I'm definitely lusting.

Instead of giving in to my urge, I take a step back and shove down my interest as I look into her hazel eyes.

"Don't let me keep you. I should get in and finish up my paperwork. Nice meeting you."

"You too."

Determined not to let those pretty eyes or that silky voice tempt me, I turn away and let myself into the office.

Despite being bone-tired, I flick on the lights and make my way to my desk. Might as well get my notes typed up for Pooja to process on Monday and get this entire frustrating file over with. At least for now.

It's my own damn fault; I should never have taken her case when she called me from jail six months ago. Krista Hardee, spoiled daughter of real estate mogul Oliver Hardee, and the woman I made the mistake of dating briefly three years ago. It hadn't taken me long to find out she was more trouble than she was worth, which was evidenced by the length of time it took me to scrape her off.

Six months ago, she'd been charged on drug trafficking charges—wrongly, she claims—and she wanted me to bond her out. It seemed like a pretty safe bet, given her father's substantial roots in the region. I frankly never considered she might jump bail.

Boy, was I wrong.

Took me a month to track her damn ass down to South Padre Island near Port Isabel, Texas. Took me another two and a half days hauling her back up here in my truck, with two decidedly unpleasant motel stays.

Fuck, was she a pain in the ass. Fought like a cat too, every chance she got. Even when I delivered her to the jail tonight, she managed to leave a mark on me.

I slip the paperwork in the folder, staple my notes to the cover for Pooja, and drop the file on her desk for Monday. For a moment, I consider going through the messages she left on my desk, but decide they'll have to wait as well.

Instead of Joe's—I might be asleep before my food is served —I end up hitting a drive-thru for a greasy burger I wolf down on my way home. After a quick shower, I throw my duffel and dirty clothes in the laundry room to deal with later, and roll into bed.

Yet instead of falling asleep right away, I lie awake for a while mulling over the case, but the last thing on my mind before I finally drift off is a pair of gorgeous hazel eyes.

Fuck.

CHAPTER TWO

Reagan

I'm wearing a big smile when I walk into the office.

"I knew you had it in the bag," Sally says, reading my expression correctly as she gets up from behind her desk. She throws her arms around me for a hug. "You nailed the bastard."

"You mean I won the case for my client," I correct her, but grin when I catch her rolling her eyes. I walk over to my desk to dump the heavy file. Sally passes on her way to the small galley kitchen in the back and returns moments later with a cake box. "Tell me that's red velvet?"

"What else?" she fires back, as she slides it on my desk before returning to the kitchen for plates and forks.

I open the familiar black and pink box from Sweet Confections on North Main. My favorite bakery and enemy to my hips. I quickly swipe through the whipped cream cheese frosting with an index finger I quickly pop in my mouth. "Oh my God," I hum around my digit, the flavor exploding on my tongue.

"You're lucky you need that finger to sign my checks," Sally grumbles, waving the chef's knife in my face before cutting a pair of decadently sized slices.

"How did you know?"

"I didn't," she admits, shrugging. "But I figured it would also serve to soothe a negative outcome had that been the case."

"Good point," I mumble, my mouth full with my first delicious bite.

For a while we eat in silence, the cake deserving every last ounce of our attention.

"So tell me," Sally finally says, using her finger to scrape the last of the icing off her plate. "How did that flatulent shitweasel react?"

I snort at her creative description for my ex. She never thought much of him to start with and, after she stood by me through my rather ugly divorce, came to hate his guts. Not that I disagree, Neil Tory absolutely *is* a shitweasel. Too bad it took me years to figure that out.

When I met him he was with the public defender's office and I'd just started with Thatcher, Cleaver, and Associates. He was an idealist then. He'd defied his father, who was the Richmond City Commonwealth Attorney, and wanted his son to follow in his footsteps, but Neil believed in defending the underdog, the vulnerable. At least he did back then, but that changed when I was making a little headway at the firm and started bringing home more money. Something his father never failed to rub in Neil's face.

That had been the beginning of the end. Our marriage crumbled and he switched sides; went from the Norfolk Public Defender's Office to his father's in Richmond two years ago. Neil, who hadn't set foot in his father's country club in years, was suddenly a member, hobnobbing with the big boys. Including my bosses. Suddenly my rise to associate came grinding to a halt and after a year of being relegated to second at the defense table, I'd had enough and handed in my resignation. I pulled up stakes in Norfolk as well and moved to smaller Suffolk to start in private practice.

The kicker was, when I took on Sean Davies' case and at the pretrial saw Neil take a seat at the prosecutor's table. That's how

I discovered he'd transferred to the Suffolk Commonwealth's Attorney's Office. For the life of me I can't figure why he's followed me here, but he seems determined to cut me down to size.

Except this time it blew up in his face.

"He looked murderous." I can still see the purple veins stand out on his forehead as he stormed out of the courtroom after the verdict was read, avoiding all eye contact.

"I bet he did," Sally cackles, and I can't help but laugh with her. "Next time I want to sit in."

"We'll see," I tell her, shaking my head as I pick up the empty plates and carry them to the kitchen. Sally follows me with the cake.

"By the way, I think they have a new guy next door." She waves herself and bats her eyelashes. "Hawt, in capital letters. Built like a Mack truck and looking like a mountain man. Did you see him?"

"That's Callum McGregor."

Her eyes widen. "McGregor? As in McGregor Bail Bonds? That McGregor?"

"That's the one," I confirm with a smile, as I slip past her to my desk where I start pulling the files from my accordion folder. "I bumped into him Friday night when I left."

Sally, who followed me, perches on the edge of my desk.

"Pray tell."

It takes me all of a minute to fill her in on the brief interaction I had with the man. I don't share I've spent a lot of my weekend playing those few minutes over and over in my head, or that I can still feel the rasp of his calloused hand against my palm. I don't subscribe to flights of fancy and can't remember the last time I fantasized about a man, if ever. Still, something must've conveyed in my voice because Sally raises her eyebrow, a smug look on her face.

"Interesting," she drawls and I recognize the tease.

"Hardly. I exchanged barely two words with the man."

"But you liked those two words," she persists, eyeing me with a keen scrutiny, reminiscent of my mother trying to poke holes in my teenage excuses.

"Shouldn't you be getting home?" I ask in an attempt to distract, looking pointedly at my watch. Lame, but it works.

"Oh, shit. What time is it? I have to take Matt to soccer practice."

"Five fifteen."

The words are barely out of my mouth when she's suddenly a flurry of activity, grabbing her belongings before running for the door.

"Later!" she yells on her way out.

The cake took care of the hunger pangs I suffered all afternoon while waiting for the jury to return a verdict, so instead of heading out for a celebratory meal for one, I sit down at my desk and sort through notes Sally left for me.

No urgent messages, but I do see she had a few calls inquiring about my services. Those I'll tackle tomorrow. I quickly jot down my billable hours for today, so she can process them into my final bill for Sean in the morning, and leave the pad with my scribbles on her desk. Then I slip into the kitchen, cut myself another slice of cake, and put it in a container to take home. In case I get hungry later.

I'm locking up behind me when the door of the bail bonds office opens and Cal McGregor is led out in handcuffs.

I hadn't even noticed the police cars.

———

CAL

"Call your brother. Please."

I tack the plea on when I see confusion in her eyes. The next moment I'm stuffed into the back of a police cruiser. Jackson will know to get in touch with Mark Phillips, one of my guys, who will get the ball rolling to get me out.

Sexual battery; that's all they said. Jesus fucking Christ.

Doesn't take a rocket scientist to figure someone didn't take too kindly to being hauled to jail. It had been a mistake to drag her back by myself. Shit, it had been a mistake to take up with her years ago, but there's nothing I can do about either of those things now.

I lay my head back on the seat and consider myself lucky I'd had the weekend to catch up on some sleep. At least I have a clear mind to deal with this.

The ride to the police station isn't long, and all too soon I find myself hustled into the familiar building.

"Sorry, Cal," Jim Shaughnessy says sympathetically when I'm led to the front desk. Jim is one of the desk sergeants I deal with on a regular basis. A friendly guy, who currently looks uncomfortable as he directs the officers down the hall to an empty interrogation room.

"Am I under arrest?" I ask again. The first time I asked, when they were slapping cuffs on me, I didn't get an answer. This time I do as they undo my cuffs and indicate for me to sit down at the small table.

"Detained for questioning. For now," the older cop, who looks vaguely familiar, finally clarifies before he and his partner leave me alone in the room.

Other than a few run-ins when I was an angry adolescent, I haven't been on this side of law enforcement and it's a little unnerving. Especially when I'm not sure my tenant will follow through on my request.

I don't have to wait long before the door opens and a detective walks in, drops a file on the table, and takes the seat across from me.

"My name is Detective Walker and I have a few questions regarding time you spent recently with Ms. Krista Hardee." He seems to be waiting for an answer, but since he hasn't really asked a question yet, I remain silent. "You are familiar with Ms. Hardee?"

"I am. As I'm sure you're aware, I dropped her off at the jail Friday night."

He nods and starts flipping through the notes in his file, occasionally humming. I know what he's doing; it's a well-known technique to make me uneasy and get me to start rambling. I'm not about to fall for it, so I cross my arms and lean back in my chair as relaxed as I can force my body to be.

"Could you unbutton your shirt for me?"

Shit. That came out of left field.

Pisses me right off but I try to keep myself under control as I slowly undo my buttons. As expected, Walker's focus is on my chest where I know the marks are still visible from when the bitch bit my pec.

"Care to tell me where you got that mark?"

I really don't and wonder if it's perhaps time to call for a lawyer when a timely knock on the door interrupts us.

Walker gets up and walks to the door, opening it a crack before he slips outside and I hear voices raised in the hallway. A minute later he comes back in.

"Your lawyer is here," he announces.

I'm confused. Even if Mark had been contacted and he'd been able to get hold of my lawyer, Milt Arenberg, it would've taken the man a while to get here from Norfolk. I have no idea who Walker is talking about until he steps out of the way, revealing Reagan Cole entering behind him.

"I'm going to need some time with my client," she says with an authority that surprises me. Her quick glance in my direction is enough for me to hold my tongue, despite the need to know what the fuck she thinks she's doing.

"We're merely looking to clarify a few things with Mr. McGregor at this point," Walker shares.

"And you're welcome to do so *after* I've had some time to confer with my client," she insists, standing her ground.

I bite my lip seeing the annoyed flare of the detective's nostrils. Reagan, on the other hand, looks calm and very composed. Jackson's little sister is clearly much more than a pretty face.

"Fine," Walker grumbles. "I'll give you a few minutes."

Reagan doesn't hesitate to take the upper hand.

"I will let you know when we're done."

The moment the door closes behind him, she turns on me.

"How do you know Jackson?" she fires off right away.

"We did our BUD/S training together."

"You're a SEAL?"

"No."

I don't add that her brother went on to finish his training, while I ended up in the hospital twenty-two weeks into the twenty-four week program with an artificial knee. The result of a training accident shattering my knee joint beyond repair. Just like that, my dreams gone up in air. It had taken me some time to get over.

She looks at me quizzically before apparently deciding there are more pressing matters at hand.

"Right, let's get to business."

But I'd like some clarifications of my own first.

"What are you doing here? Where is Milt?"

"I followed you here, and who's Milt?"

"My lawyer, Milt Arenberg."

"Oh. I got a call from Mark—Jackson must've given him my number—asking me to jump in. Apparently Arenberg is out of the country. Something about a safari in Kenya, not sure. Anyway, I'm here. All the desk sergeant would tell me was they're questioning you in relation to a sexual battery case. Tell me what that has to do with you." She looks at me sharply. "I need to know everything."

The last thing I want to do is explain my history with Krista to this woman, but it looks like I have little choice.

CHAPTER THREE

Reagan

Holy shit.

I glance at the man beside me. I have to give it to him; he makes no effort to avoid my scrutiny as he buttons up his shirt. That fading bite mark looked pretty damning.

"You had a relationship with this woman."

"I wouldn't call it that. I saw her for a brief period a long time ago, and then it ended. Didn't hear from her in years until she called me out of the blue, six months or so ago. She'd been arrested and charged with drug trafficking."

"Did that surprise you?"

"Which one? That she called me or that she was peddling drugs?" His retort is sharp: a challenge.

"Her call," I clarify calmly.

Don't ask me why, but I sense he's not one who'd knowingly associate with anyone involved with drugs. After fourteen years as a defense lawyer, my instincts are well honed and they tell me Callum McGregor is a straight shooter.

"To be honest, both surprised me."

"But you bailed her out." I look up from the yellow pad I've been scribbling notes on.

"I did. Her father paid the bond and given his status in this community, I felt she was a safe bet. No other reason than that," he adds, looking at me pointedly.

"Go on," I prompt him.

"She checked in on her assigned dates and then one day, a little over a month ago, she didn't. She'd bailed." His eyes drift to the wall as he rubs his chin, and I note that sometime during the weekend he'd had time to get his hair and beard trimmed. "Daddy claimed not to know where she went and I was inclined to believe him. He stood to lose a whack of money if she couldn't be found."

"But you did find her."

"Eventually. In Texas; South Padre Island."

I hum and scribble some more notes down before looking up at him.

"How did you get her back here?"

"Drove."

"All the way through?"

I get another glare, but that doesn't bother me. He'll eventually get asked about that. We're not exactly talking about a few hours' drive.

"Stopped at a motel both Wednesday and Thursday night. And before you ask, she was cuffed to the bed and I sat up in a chair."

I nod, jotting down some details and without looking up, I shoot off my next question, "So how'd you get the bite?"

"Krista. She wasn't too keen on coming with me. The bite was her last ditch effort when I was getting her out of the car at the jail."

Again he meets my eyes straight on and there is no sign of deceit in his. I believe him.

"Okay." I put down my pen and fold my hands in front of me on the table. "Why do you think she'd make a claim like this?"

"Got no clue. She's pissed at me?"

Could be, but I get the sense that's not all there is to it.

"Let's find out," I suggest, as I get up and walk to the door.

"Keep your answers short and to the point. Don't elaborate. Make them ask the questions," I instruct him before opening the door to Detective Walker. "Ask your questions, Detective."

With a displeased scowl on his face, Walker enters the room.

It's after ten by the time we walk out of the police station, my stomach rumbling again. I have a tendency to forget about eating when I'm busy, only to binge eat when I get home or pick up unhealthy food on the way. The container with the slice of cake I took from the office will have to wait until I get home, though, since I offered to give the big man lumbering beside me a ride before my brain was able to engage.

I've decided I'm not a fan of Detective Walker, who just spent almost three hours grilling my client. An interview I tried to call to a halt several times, but my new client insisted he wanted to 'get it over with.' Walker had been especially interested in the bite mark on Cal's chest, even taking some pictures for his file.

"This is us," I tell Cal when I use the remote key to unlock the doors to my Kia Soul.

Cal stops in his tracks and stares at my vehicle.

"That's your car?"

By way of answer, I open the driver's side door and slide inside, clearing off the passenger seat and waiting for him to get in the other side. I have to keep myself from snickering when he folds himself into what I always considered to be a surprisingly roomy car. It suddenly feels cramped in here.

"So that was a good catch," I compliment him, in an effort to distract myself and him from the close quarters. I look at him as I start the engine. "The security cameras at the jail, I mean."

Cal pointed out as the detective was taking pictures there were bound to be cameras aimed at the parking lot that would show what actually went down when the woman latched onto him with her teeth.

"Don't think Walker was too impressed," he grumbles.

"Detective Walker appears to have his own agenda," I agree, "but he can't ignore the lead."

"Thanks." I turn to him and find him looking at me. "For stepping in," he adds.

"No problem. So, I assume your vehicle is back at the office?"

Before he can answer, my empty stomach loudly announces its displeasure and Cal starts laughing.

"Do you ever eat?" he asks, studying my mortified expression with amused interest.

"On occasion," I respond primly.

"Good. I'm starving too. Hope you like Mexican, because I've been craving Joe's for weeks."

"Oh, I don't think—"

"Take the next right," he interrupts.

I open my mouth to object but think better of it when another embarrassing hungry rumble sounds. What can I say; I'm a sucker for Mexican.

———

CAL

"Can I get you anything else?"

Reagan smiles at the waitress as she sits back and pats her stomach.

"I couldn't if I tried."

"Just the bill, please," I jump in.

We made it here just in time. Joe's kitchen usually stays open until eleven to cater to the patrons of some of the surrounding bars. We ordered finger food instead of individual meals, and I was surprised to see Reagan managed to wolf down her fair share. I'd much rather see that than sit across from a woman who plays around with a few lettuce leaves. She also likes beer, which I consider to be another bonus.

Heck, if she weren't Jackson's sister, she'd be fucking perfection. Not too short or too tall; a spectacular ass; that long, shiny, dark hair, and not to mention those eyes. Add to that a sense of humor, keen intelligence, and considerable confidence, and you have my dream woman.

Shit.

I intercept the bill the moment I see her grabbing for her purse when the waitress returns. I ignore her pointed look as I tuck a few bills under my glass, leaving a healthy tip for the waitress.

"Consider it a retainer." I get up and grin when I catch her shaking her head.

Putting a hand in the small of her back, I lead her through the maze of empty tables to the door.

"I would've pegged you for a luxury vehicle," I point out when we get to the parking lot.

"When I started up on my own it was the Lexus or Sally— she's my paralegal," she explains.

"I see Sally won."

"She did and for the record, I actually like my little Soul."

She throws me a meaningful glance before unlocking the doors and getting in. I wisely keep my mouth shut until we pull out of the parking lot.

"Your brother told me you left Thatcher, Cleaver, and Associates to strike out on your own. What precipitated that move?"

"He did, did he?" She glances at me and I can tell it isn't a subject she's comfortable discussing, which makes me even more curious. When I keep my eyes on her and my mouth closed, she finally concedes, "It ended up being a dead-end street for me."

"I see," I volunteer. I'm pretty sure there's more to that story but it'll keep. I'm intrigued by her and if it were up to me, there would be plenty of occasions to dig a little deeper.

"When did he tell you that? Jackson."

Guess it's fair turnaround she does a little digging of her own.

I could play dumb, but chances are this will come out at some point, regardless, so I may as well get ahead of the curve.

"When he called to see if I knew of an office space for rent."

I catch her eyes narrowing and her hands tighten on the steering wheel.

"For me."

It was more of a statement than a question, but I answer anyway.

"Yup."

"And you happened to have an empty office beside yours?"

"Sort of."

Suddenly I feel put on the spot. I'm sure her brother had a reason not to tell her about our connection, but I'm not privy to it. Rock, meet hard place.

She turns into the parking lot in front of our building and turns the engine off. I can feel her eyes on me.

"Sort of?"

"The previous tenant was delinquent on his rent. I'd been lenient too long already." I keep the fact her brother paid off any outstanding rent the real estate agent owed me, in return for him to vacate the premises in days. Fucking Jackson can tell her himself.

"Just like that?"

"Just like that," I confirm, opening the car door and unfolding myself. After I close the door, I realize she hasn't moved. I walk around to the driver's side, motioning for her to lower the window, leaning down so we're at eye level.

"Appreciate this. I'll pop by tomorrow to settle with you."

She huffs and waves me off. "Don't worry about that yet. We should sit down and strategize, though, so whenever you have some time you could spare, I'll be in the office most of the day."

"Strategize? You don't think this is the end of it?"

She shrugs. "It's possible, but something tells me Detective Walker will be back. I hope for the best, but experience has taught me I should plan for the worst."

I wonder what kind of experience would have netted her that lesson.

"I'll drop by," I promise. I likely would've anyway and that has nothing to do with this bogus charge and everything to do with her. "It's late, you should head home."

She smiles at me. Fuck, she's gorgeous.

"Now you sound like my brother."

Oh, hell no. I stick my face a little farther into the open window.

"Trust me, I'm nothing like your brother," I promise, and she sucks in a sharp little breath, drawing my eyes to her mouth. I notice a small streak of red in the corner. Salsa, I suspect.

"Thanks for dinner."

Her voice is a little hoarse and against better judgment I reach in the window. With my thumb I brush her plump bottom lip before cleaning the spot.

"You're wearing it."

Immediately she starts wiping at her mouth, but those eyes stay on me. If I don't get out of here now, I'm going to do something I'll regret.

"And it was my pleasure."

I rap my knuckles on her roof and head toward my vehicle. It's the smart thing to do.

CHAPTER FOUR

Reagan

Feels like spring out here.

It's not often I take my time in the morning, but it was a late night last night and it took me a while to get to sleep. I let the early morning sun kiss my face.

I already talked to Sally and let her know I'd be in by ten. She's warned that should Cal show up, she'll make my apologies. Of course that prompted some questions, but I was able to avoid getting into it over the phone with a promise I'd fill her in when I got there.

With my feet propped up on the deck railing, I look out over my backyard and the swamp beyond. I bought this old farmhouse when Neil and I split and sold the marital home in downtown Norfolk. Sadly I haven't had much time to enjoy it.

I've always wanted to live in the country. Somewhere I could put down roots, maybe have a few animals. Growing up a military brat—my dad was an Air Force pilot—my mom had her hands full raising my brother and me, basically on her own. There was no way she was going to add animals to the mix.

Ironically, I've lived here for almost two years and still don't have a single animal—not even a goldfish—because I'm afraid

I'm too busy to look after it. I'm wondering if being too busy is always going to be an excuse for me.

I take a sip of my coffee and watch a flock of birds settle in the treetops, a melancholy feeling pressing on my chest.

Neil and I never had kids for the same reason; too busy. What didn't help was he'd wanted kids but expected me to sacrifice my career for it. I'd always dreamed parenting would be something you did together, as a team, but not my ex. So in the end I may have wanted children, but certainly not with someone who had no plans to contribute other than sperm.

Okay, now I'm just making myself miserable with those depressing thoughts. I throw back the dregs of my coffee and make my way inside, closing and locking the sliding door behind me.

I'm in my car on the way to the office when my brother calls.

"Morning."

"What happened? Waited all night for your call."

"Well, hello to you too," I snap, my bristles up at his agitated tone.

There's a pointed silence before his voice is back, a tad more moderate.

"Morning, Sis. Did you get things sorted last night?"

"For the time being anyway."

"Took long enough. I tried calling a few times."

"Yeah, I had my phone turned off at the police station and forgot to turn it back on until I got home."

"So fill me in?" he asks.

I hesitate; he may be my brother, but it's not my place to discuss my client's business with him and for now, Cal is the client.

"Reagan?"

"Don't feel comfortable discussing this with you, Jackson. I mean, I know he's supposed to be your friend, but I'd never heard his name from your mouth until last night."

"Of course you have," Jackson insists.

"Pretty sure I would've remembered."

"I'm sure I've mentioned Mac before."

"Mac? Cal is Mac?"

I remember Jackson talking about Mac, a buddy whose leg was crushed during BUD/S training. I can vaguely recall a couple of other times his name was mentioned, but I'd never met the guy.

"One and the same. We've kept in touch over the years and he occasionally does some work for Cole Security."

That's Jackson's security firm here in Virginia. It shouldn't surprise me Cal has a call sign; most of the guys working with Jackson do. Hell, Jackson himself is known as Muff or Muffin. He still hasn't shared what earned him that title, but maybe I can convince Cal to tell me.

"Good, then you can call him yourself to find out what happened." I stick to my guns.

"Always playing by the rules," he teases.

"You know it."

I grin when I hear his exaggerated sigh.

"I'm at the office, Brother-dear. I should get going. Give my love to Catherine and the girls."

"Fine, blow me off."

I pull the car into my slot and turn off the engine, grabbing my phone from the dock and putting it to my ear as I get out of the car.

"Finally he clues in," it's my turn to tease.

"Jesus, when did you grow into such a hard-ass?"

"Since I wiped the courtroom with my ex."

Jackson barks out a laugh. "You won? You beat the bastard?"

My brother never was a fan of Neil Tory. I believe he may have been the first one to call him a snake-eyed shyster, a term I've used quite a few times myself in the past years.

"I got my client an acquittal, yes," I confirm, more modestly than my shit-eating grin implies.

"Atta girl, Sis. Gonna have to celebrate soon."

"I'm game if you're buying. I'm at the office, I've gotta go."

"Okay, I'll give Cal a call. Later, Sis."

"Later."

I'm still smiling when I walk into the office to find Sally chatting with Sean Davies, who is holding a big bouquet of flowers.

"There she is," Sally points out unnecessarily. "Sean came by to pay his bill."

My client is in his mid-fifties and owns a small trucking company. He's not without means or charm—a handsome enough silver fox, or so he likes to describe himself—but neither his money nor his charm has worked on me. He's tried. I've had to remind him gently several times as his lawyer it would be inappropriate, if not downright unethical, for me to go on a date with him. Never mind the fact I'm not interested, certainly not in someone who hits up bars to pick up hookers.

Unfortunately, it looks like I've been a little too gentle, as Sean presses the opulent bouquet in my hands.

"I thought we should celebrate," he starts, and I dart a look over his shoulder at a wide-eyed Sally. "The invoice is settled and technically you're no longer my—"

I hold up my hand to stop him, guessing where this is going to go.

"That's kind of you. Sally and I are happy with the outcome of your case. I certainly hope you won't need our services again."

His face drops and he looks crestfallen at my veiled dismissal.

"Of course," he quickly catches himself. "I just thought...I'm uh..."

"Here," Sally jumps in, grabbing the flowers from my hand. "Let me get those in some water. Oh, and, Reagan? Mr. McGregor should be here shortly."

I could kiss her for rescuing me from this uncomfortable standoff and I grab onto the cue she's handed me.

"Yes, thank you for reminding me." I turn to Sean and hold out my hand. "Well, I should prepare for that meeting, but thank you for the flowers, they'll cheer up our office."

He shakes my hand and opens his mouth before closing it again with a nod. I think the penny has dropped.

I watch him leave the office before turning back to find Sally sticking her head out of the kitchen.

"Sorry. I didn't have a chance to give you the heads-up."

"No worries. I think he got the message."

"I wouldn't be so sure." She grimaces and sets the vase on my desk. "Found this in the bouquet," she says, pointing at a small card tucked in the flowers.

I fold it open and groan when I read what is written.

Hope we see each other again. Soon.
Yours, Sean

"Oh, shit," Sally snorts.

"My thoughts exactly."

———

CAL

I came in early; trying to get a head start before Mark Phillips, one of my bondsmen, and Pooja Bahri, my office manager, came in and I'd had to explain what happened last night. I barely got done with that when Jackson called, and I ended up going over everything again with him.

Apparently he tried his sister first, who waved client privilege in his face. That gets a chuckle out of me, especially since he sounds disgruntled by her refusal to share.

It does give me an opening to talk a little about her.

"She seems to know her stuff, your sister."

"She sure does." He chuckles. "People make the mistake of

taking her at face value—pretty girl with those big innocent eyes —little do they know a shark lives underneath."

"Good to know I have her in my corner, then."

"You couldn't do any better than Reagan," he confirms with something more than only brotherly pride, but I can't quite put my finger on it. Then his tone changes. "Something that fuck-tard of a husband of hers was too dumb to see."

"Husband?" I echo, trying hard to keep the disappointment out of my voice.

"Ex," he clarifies and I let out a relieved breath. "Divorced his ass a couple of years ago, but the guy is like a burr that won't let go. He already made her life miserable but apparently still isn't done."

I'd love to dig deeper but I'm afraid I'll tip my hand—something I'd like to avoid—and besides, I don't think Reagan would appreciate me going behind her back for information.

"Anyway," Jackson continues, "you can trust her; she'll look after you."

"Thanks, Muff, appreciate it. I should get going, got stuff to do."

I don't tell him the 'stuff' I'm referring to is going next door to see his sister.

The first thing I see, when I walk in the door of her office, is the massive bouquet of flowers on the corner of a desk I peg as Reagan's because of the stacks of folders, but she's not at it.

"Hi." A short rounded woman with light-brown, spiky hair sticking up every which way and heavy-rimmed glasses leans over her desk and holds out her hand. "I'm Sally, Reagan's assistant. And you are Callum McGregor." I take her hand and raise an eyebrow. "Reagan told me who you were."

"Nice to meet you. Is she...uh...around?"

"She's just finishing up a call in the conference room. She shouldn't be long, why don't you have a seat?"

She indicates a couple of visitors' chairs in front of Reagan's desk and I walk over, casually checking out the flowers in passing and noting a small card. The flowers intrigue me and I take the seat closest to them, attempting to read what's on the card. The only thing I can decipher is a signature scribbled at the bottom, and I wonder who the fuck Sean is and what he is to Reagan.

"Hey."

I snap my head around to find her standing right beside me. I wonder if she caught me checking out the card.

"Morning. I was just checking out your flowers."

"Happy client," she says with a shrug.

Behind me I hear her assistant stifle a snort.

"Must be," I conclude, catching a twitch at the corner of Reagan's mouth.

"Want some coffee?"

"Sure."

"Sally..."

"Got it," her assistant chirps.

"We'll be in the conference room."

I bite down a grin at the term conference room for a space that barely holds what looks like a round dining table, dotted with more folders and paperwork. She quickly stacks them and shoves them to one side before putting a yellow pad in front of her.

"If you don't mind," she starts, "I want to go over the notes I made last night to ensure I got it down correctly. I plan to check in with Detective Walker sometime today. Hopefully he'll have had a chance to look at the jail's video feed, but I want to be well prepared in case it doesn't show what we hope it will."

It takes us close to an hour to go over all of her notes, with the only interruption Sally, who brought us coffee. I was able to fill in a few blanks with names, dates, and places where we stopped or stayed on our way back from Texas.

"I think that's all for now, if I come across anything else, I'll give you a call."

"Is that a roundabout way to get my number?" I tease.

A deep blush creeps up on her cheeks. Funny how such a strong and competent woman can still be affected by a little flirting. It only makes her more attractive—and dangerous.

I reach across the table for her pen and paper, and scribble down my cell number before sliding both back to her. She ducks her head and puts aside the pad before shoving back from the table. I get up as well.

"We didn't discuss fees yet," I point out.

"We will if it turns out you need me," she dismisses, walking out of the room.

When I follow her into the front office I notice that damn bouquet on her desk.

"Maybe I should be getting you flowers as a thank you?"

Her eyes shoot to her desk before she turns them on me, laugh lines appearing at the corners.

"Not necessary."

"Perfect; dinner it is."

I'm not sure what prompted me to say that. Actually, that's a lie; I know exactly what prompted me. It's still probably a really bad idea, but I'm caring less about that with each moment I spend in her presence.

I catch Sally's grinning thumbs-up behind her boss's back as Reagan shakes her head, trying to catch up. At least I have one cheerleader.

"Wait, I never said—" Reagan sputters.

I spot one of those little business card holders on her desk and fish one out. It lists both her office and cell phone numbers.

"Now I have your number too," I tease. "I'll call."

Sally's hearty chuckle follows me out the door.

CHAPTER FIVE

Reagan

"Way to go, Matt!"

Sally whistles on her fingers, a talent I don't have, so I simply stand and clap as her son is surrounded by his teammates, who are slapping him on the back.

I'm sure my family would get a kick out of me at a kid's soccer game, given that I avoided sports like the plague growing up. I wouldn't be here if Sally's boy hadn't begged me to come. That was last night, over the pizza I invited them out to. He'd been telling me how excited he was for his first game of the season and I guess I showed a little too much enthusiasm, because the next thing I knew he was pleading with me to come watch. I didn't have the heart to disappoint him.

So here I am, leaving the office early just so I could be here for kickoff.

He's a good kid, and apparently a good player; something I only know because he just scored a goal. I'm sports illiterate. I can barely keep track of the ball with clusters of kids running from one end of the field to the other without much rhyme or reason—at least to me.

I follow suit and sit down like everyone else does when I feel my phone buzzing in my pocket. Again. I've ignored two previous calls, wanting to give the game my full attention, but whoever is calling seems to need my attention urgently. My thoughts go to my parents, who moved to Arizona a few years ago, and Dad has had some health issues lately.

"I'll be right back," I inform Sally, making my way down the rickety bleachers and away from the soccer field.

The same number called all three times, but it's not one I'm familiar with. No voicemails but a text from the same number.

Unknown: Where are you?

I'm trying to think who might be looking for me who isn't on my contact list.

Me: Who is this?

I've barely hit send when the phone buzzes again, and this time I answer, but I don't get a chance to say anything.

"Came looking for you and the office was closed."

"Cal?"

I haven't seen or spoken to him since Tuesday. There hadn't been anything to report, I'm still waiting for a call back from Detective Walker about the surveillance camera feeds. I left him a couple of messages with my office number but he doesn't seem to be inclined to get back to me. I hoped in this case no news was good news and perhaps the tapes exonerated my client.

I'll admit, I've stared out the front window at the office more than is my norm—maybe trying to catch a glimpse—but I've mostly squashed my irrational attraction to him. For all intents and purposes he's a client, and like I told Sean just the other day, it would be highly inappropriate to even engage in anything but a professional manner with Cal.

I hear his deep chuckle before he repeats, "Where are you?" and it annoys me.

"You know, there is such a thing as telephone etiquette where you allow the person you're contacting to actually *answer* the call before you start talking. Also, since when is it your business when I close my office or where I go?"

That seems to silence him. For a second or two.

"Right. Well, I'll do my best next time to exercise *telephone etiquette*—" The sarcasm is thick and I can hear the finger quotes in his voice. "But I'll warn you now, it's never been a strong suit. Phone calls are, in my opinion, a necessary evil not intended for inane chitchat and only good for conveying information. Right now the information I'm looking for is your current location."

I have a hard time hanging onto my snit and find myself snorting at his disgruntled rant.

"So noted. No leisurely late night chats for you. I'll keep that in mind."

I'm playing with fire and I know it. Still, I can't seem to help myself.

"Wait. I didn't say—"

Now I'm laughing out loud and quickly volunteer, "The soccer field at Lakeland High School."

I wince the moment the words are out of my mouth. *What are you doing, Reagan?*

"What are you doing there?"

"Watching twenty-two ten-year-olds chasing a ball around."

There's a pause.

"Muff never mentioned you had a kid."

"Not mine. Sally's boy, Matt." It sounds suspiciously like a relieved breath on the other side, and I can't help probe a little. "Not a fan of kids?"

"I didn't say that. I like kids well enough, but we're getting off topic here."

"Which was?" I prompt, since I'm still not clear what he's calling for.

"Dinner, but we can talk about that when I get there."

"Where? Here?"

There is no answer, just dead air. He's already gone.

Sally is looking for me when I start up the bleachers.

"Everything okay?"

"It's fine."

I sit down and try to avoid her scrutiny by pretending to watch the game.

"Is that why you look like someone kicked your puppy?" she persists.

Yeah, figured it was too much to hope for her to let it drop. I close my eyes and sigh deeply.

"Cal was looking for me."

Sally lets out a little squeal and shoves my shoulder. I give her a dirty look.

"Honestly, I can't for the life of me understand why that would upset you. I would give my firstborn to have a man like that looking for me."

"First of all, your firstborn is your only child, and secondly; you would never," I counter. "You love that kid."

"I won't love him that much when he climbs in the back of my car after the game smelling like the bottom of a dumpster," she shoots back.

"You're full of it. Anyway," I get us back on track, "I think he's on his way here."

That earns me another squeal but she is quickly distracted by something happening on the field. The next moment she's on her feet, cheering on her son, who appears to be running for the goal and ends up scoring again.

As I get to my feet to join in the cheers, I glance over and catch Cal's truck pulling into the parking lot. My eyes are locked on him as he gets out and starts walking in our direction. His gait is relaxed; limber even, as his long legs eat up the distance. About halfway to the bleachers, his eyes come up and catch on me.

I don't even notice everyone around me is already sitting until Cal starts climbing up the stands.

———

CAL

A dark blush stains her cheeks as she drops down in her seat. I fucking love I seem to impact her as much as she does me.

My common sense takes a flying leap when it comes to Reagan Cole. I know it's gonna blow up in my face at some point, but I still can't seem to keep myself away.

She avoids looking at me when I sit down beside her.

"Hey, Cal," Sally greets me, and I lean forward to look beyond Reagan.

"Sally. Your boy out there?"

"Blue team, he plays forward." I glance over at the field and spot the kid she's pointing at. "He just scored," she adds proudly.

"Good for him." Switching my attention to the woman beside me, I give her a little nudge. "Didn't take you for a soccer fan."

She turns those eyes on me. "I'm not. Not really. I'm more of a Matt fan."

That says a lot about her, all of it good.

I open my mouth to ask her about dinner when two sharp whistles sound from the field, ending the game. We get swept along when the bleachers clear and wait by the fence until Sally's son comes running off the field. He ignores his mom and throws himself at Reagan, who grins from ear to ear.

"Did you see me, Auntie Reagan? Did you see my goal?"

"Sure did. Both of them," she says, setting the boy back as her face scrunches up. "You did really well."

"What am I? Chopped liver?" Sally complains, and her son turns to hug her as well. "Whoa, buddy. You're particularly ripe today," she says, making a face much like Reagan's. "Go grab your bag and we'll roll down the windows on the way home."

"Who are you?" Matt stops in front of me and looks up.

"That's Cal; Auntie Reagan's friend. Now get going and we'll pick up a couple of burgers on the way home."

The boy glares at me before turning a smile on Reagan.

"You wanna come have burgers with us, Auntie Reagan?"

I duck my head and grin. Apparently the kid has good taste.

"I'd love to—" she starts to answer, but I quickly jump in.

"But she can't tonight. We already have plans." I ignore her sharp glare. "Nice to meet you, though," I add, winking at Sally as I take Reagan by the elbow and steer her to my truck.

"My car is over there." She pulls at my hold on her arm.

"I'll drop you off here after dinner."

"I can't go out to dinner. I reek of boy sweat," she complains, plucking at her sticky shirt.

"I don't care, I'm used to it," I offer, but that doesn't seem to fly as her eyes narrow and she plants her fists on her hips.

"Well, I'm not and I don't want to go anywhere sticky with someone else's sweat."

I quickly bend my head and stare at my boots, because the mental image she paints has my blood heat in an instant. Reagan naked, flushed, and slicked with sweat. I clear my throat before I look up.

"Change of plans. Go home, do what you need to do, and I'll be there in thirty with dinner."

I click the remote and open my driver's side door while she processes the information.

"I don't think—"

"Indian okay?"

"I love Indian, but—"

"Excellent. I'll pick up some butter chicken and naan."

Before she has a chance to say anything else, I get in behind the wheel and close the door. When I drive off the parking lot, I glance in my rearview mirror to see her still standing in the same spot, glaring at me.

This is going to be fun.

It's more like forty-five minutes by the time I pull up to the old farmhouse.

Finding her address had taken me all of five minutes while waiting for my order to be ready. I'd expected to find her living in one of the newer developments in town and was surprised to see the rural address. Right on the edge of the Great Dismal Swamp Wildlife Refuge, on a fair bit of land, judging from the length of her dirt driveway. The house itself is quaint, with dark red siding and crisp white trim. I'm guessing it was fixed up not too long ago. A large porch wraps around the front and halfway down each side, trimmed with a wide flowerbed. Brick steps go up the center to a rustic front door framed by two cast iron lanterns.

The place doesn't quite seem to match the classy, and well put-together attorney.

I pull my truck up to the detached ramshackle garage, and park it next to that toy car she drives. I grab the paper bag with food and make my way over to the house and up the steps.

I'm starting to wonder if she's going to leave me standing here—after knocking for the second time—when suddenly the door opens.

The woman in front of me looks like she belongs here; the shiny straight hair now wet and pinned in a sloppy bun on top of her head, and the sleek, professional suit and pumps replaced with a pair of ripped jeans, a flannel shirt, and pretty bare feet tipped with deep red painted nails. There isn't a speck of makeup on her face and I'll be damned if she doesn't look even more beautiful this way.

"Wasn't sure you were gonna open the door."

"To be honest, I wasn't sure myself," she answers, sounding a bit breathless. Then she steps aside. "You may as well come in."

Not the warmest invitation I've ever received, but it's definitely the most welcome one.

There's a stairway going up to the second floor straight ahead, what looks like an office to my right, and on the left a large open space holding living and dining room. She closes the door and leads the way to the back where the dining room opens up to the kitchen, which is tucked behind the stairs.

The view from the picture windows is fantastic; a garden, maybe fifty-or-so-feet deep where it ends and the swamp begins.

"Quite the view you have here," I comment, hearing cupboards opening and closing behind me.

"It's the reason I got the place," she volunteers, and I turn around to find her staring dreamily out the window. "I always wanted to live somewhere remote, but there isn't much use for lawyers out in the boonies. This is the best of both worlds; I get to look at this every day and live only fifteen minutes from the city."

"For sure. Do you get a lot of wildlife?"

I set the bag on the table and unpack the food.

"Deer, mostly. Although a few black bear as well. Last fall I had one on my deck." She laughs a little. "Almost fainted when I walked into the kitchen and he was standing up against the sliding door. He eventually left. Probably just looking for food to fatten up on before winter."

"That'd be a bit of a scare," I concede.

"Yeah, it had me go out and get some protection for when I go outside. Just in case."

I envision Reagan toting a shotgun, but she points at the odd-shaped canister on the counter by the back door and I chuckle.

"An air horn?"

She grins back at me. "Works like a charm. I chased one off earlier this year. May have even been the same one, I don't know, but he ran when I blasted that thing out the back door."

"I bet. Where do you want the food?"

"Dining table?" She hands me a cork mat and I set the dishes on top in the middle of the table. "What would you like to drink?"

"You got beer?"

That earns me a raised eyebrow before she dives into a well-stocked fridge with a door full of beer bottles. This woman is turning into more of a dream every second.

I'm fucked.

I close in behind her, so when she straightens up and turns around, I'm inches away. I take the beers from her hands and set them on the counter. Then I hook a hand behind her neck and pull her close, her hazel eyes widening as I lean down.

"What are you doing?" she whispers breathlessly.

"I'm just speeding along what we both know is inevitable."

Her mouth opens on a small gasp and I take my opportunity, closing my mouth over hers.

Oh yeah, I'm so fucked.

CHAPTER SIX

Reagan

Sweet baby Jesus, the man can kiss.

"Whoa," escapes me when he lets me up for air and my eyes blink open.

"No shit." His eyes sparkle with humor and right underneath I can still see heat simmer. He brushes a thumb over my swollen lips before he steps back. "Let's eat before I'm tempted to satisfy my appetite another way."

I suck in a breath and immediately feel the flush on my cheeks heating. This man is my client, I'm his lawyer, this should not have happened, and yet I have a flock of happy butterflies in my stomach. I abruptly turn and busy myself digging through drawers for cutlery and serving spoons, while trying to get a handle on my runaway libido. Christ, you'd think I hit perimenopause with the intense responses my body seems to experience around him.

When I finally turn around, he's already sitting at the dining table—his back to me—taking a deep tug of his beer. The other bottle is waiting for me across from him. Shoring up my proverbial panties, I go and join him.

During dinner I steer the conversation into safer waters—my

brother, BUD/S training, clients we have in common— anything but what happened in the kitchen.

"So good," I mumble around a mouthful of naan, which I slopped around in the remaining butter chicken sauce on my plate. "Glad these jeans are roomy."

I look up at Cal's deep chuckle. He's leaning back in his chair, taking a sip of his bottle while observing me.

"What? Do I have food on my face?" I start wiping with my napkin but he shakes his head.

"No." He shrugs. "I like watching you eat."

Lovely, just what every girl wants to hear.

I know I wolf down food. Heck, growing up with an older brother, it was the only way to ensure what was on *my* plate actually ended up in *my* stomach. These days it's more about not having, or taking, the time savoring what I eat. Don't get me wrong, I enjoy food as much as the next person—maybe even a little too much—I'm just used to shoveling it down as fast as I can

"That's not weird at all," I deflect my own uneasiness with sarcasm, as I stand and start gathering up dishes.

He grabs the rest and follows me into the kitchen where I already have the water running in the sink. I have a dishwasher, but rarely use it; I much prefer to hand-wash my dishes. It's relaxing, with my hands in warm water, letting my mind go as I stare out the window.

"Got plans this weekend?"

Cal is casually leaning against the counter, a dish towel in hand, his hand out for the next plate. Could he be any more attractive? He's so different from my ex, so unlike any of the preppy, clean-cut guys I dated in college—*so* not my type. Or maybe he's exactly that and I'm wading into very hot water.

I take him in; those long legs cast in well-worn jeans, a gray Henley, that beard, and then the unkempt hair almost covering his dark eyes. Those eyes are currently looking at me keenly, and I remember I owe him an answer.

"Uh...I've got some work to finish and do my regular weekend stuff."

He raises an eyebrow, the corner of his mouth twitching.

"Regular weekend stuff?"

"Normal stuff; groceries, laundry, gardening."

He looks over his shoulder at my backyard. "You do all of that yourself? I wouldn't have guessed that."

"I enjoy it. It's relaxing," I respond, a little defensively which earns me an immediate wide grin.

"Not dissing it. I've barely had a chance to get used to you without your professional armor, knowing you like getting your hands dirty only adds to the appeal." Dammit, now I'm turning beet red again. I quickly duck my head and focus on the dishes, but he reaches over and brushes a stray hank of hair behind my ear. "That blush is cute as fuck too. You know there are ways other than gardening to relax, right?" he flirts, and my body responds with a delicious shiver that has the hair on my arms stand up.

"You're not helping," I grumble, rinsing and draining the sink. When I turn to wipe my hands, I try not to notice the smoldering look in his eyes. In an attempt to throw cold water on the fire he's stoking, I bring up my brother. "So, Jackson told me you're the Mac he used to talk about."

My attempt at diversion appears to work when he straightens and his gaze drifts out the window, but not before I observe him flinch.

"Yeah. They called me Mac." His eyes come back to me, and the heat I saw there before has cooled down significantly. "What did he tell you about me?"

"I remember him mentioning you were badly injured in a training accident. Your leg?" He nods, his hand inadvertently reaching down to rub his left leg. "Is that why you didn't become a SEAL?"

"Artificial knees don't work well for SEALs."

There's bitterness in his voice and I instinctively reach out and put my hand on his arm. He pulls back like he got burned, startling me.

"I'm sorry," I mutter, afraid I've overstepped.

"No need to be." His mouth twitches into a self-deprecating smile. "I probably wouldn't have held up under all that structure anyway. It all worked out. My training and my size got me a job working for my uncle. He was a bail bondsman in Richmond." He shrugs. "The rest is history."

"Does it still bother you?"

"My knee? Nah, it gets tight from time to time and I've learned to avoid landing on it, but other than that, it's become just another part of my body."

His smile is friendly, but something is different. Suddenly unsure what to say, I turn to my Keurig.

"I'm gonna make some coffee, do you want one?"

"Sure, but I should probably take it to go."

I'm glad I have my back turned so he can't read the disappointment on my face.

"Okay."

"Reagan..."

"Regular or decaf?" I quickly ask, my voice a bit squeaky.

I reach up to grab a travel mug from the top shelf when I feel the heat of his body right behind me.

"I've got it," he says, his breath brushing my cheek as he easily picks a mug and sets it down on the counter in front of me. But he doesn't move, and I'm afraid to breathe.

When I finally feel him step away and try to focus on setting up the Keurig, my hands are shaking.

Five minutes later I'm showing him the door, and he surprises me with a brief hard kiss on my lips before he marches to his truck without a word.

———

CAL

Shit.

I rub a hand over my face at the sound of my alarm. It had taken a while for me to fall asleep.

I bailed last night, all but ran from Reagan's place with the excuse I had some work left to do. The damn coffee she handed me is still in my truck—cold by now—but that goodbye kiss I stole from her still burns on my lips.

God knows what she must be thinking; I went from hot to cold in the time it took her to mention Jackson's name, who I'd conveniently relegated far to the background. The reminder made me realize I at least owe the man a heads-up I'm interested in his sister. He won't like it and there's nothing I can do about that, but he needs to know I intend to see her.

Of course, after last night, she may not be as receptive, but we'll cross that bridge when we get to it.

I swing my legs out of bed and get started on my day. There's work waiting for me at the office.

Aaron Morales, who goes by Moe, looks up when I walk in.

"You're early," I point out, throwing my keys and phone on my desk before sitting down.

"I know. Got a call from Troy Jensen's mother an hour ago. She says she went to check on him this morning, and it looks like he packed a few things and took off. His truck's gone too."

"Fuck!"

The armed robbery trial for the twenty-two-year-old punk is scheduled to start next week. We've been keeping close tabs on him with the help of his mother, who had to take out a second mortgage on her house to pay his bond. The kid's been a squirrely pain in the ass from day one.

"I'm just here to pull all the contacts I have for him before I head out," Moe explains, Troy's file open in front of him.

"Do you need backup?" It would mean my own work would have to wait, but that can't be helped.

"I'm good. I've got Mark on standby, should I need an extra hand."

I nod my understanding and turn to the constant pile of paperwork on my desk. It seems every time I think I'm making a dent new files appear.

I'm buried so deep in my work I barely acknowledge Moe when he takes off, calling out a rushed goodbye, but for some reason I clearly hear it when someone enters the office next door a couple of hours later. A quick glance out the window shows Reagan's toy car in the parking lot, and just like that my concentration is shot.

Sitting back down at my desk, I grab my phone and find Muff's number in my contacts. His cell phone rings five times before going into voicemail. Instead of leaving a message, I find his home number and try again with the same result.

Shit. I was hoping to have this dealt with before going next door. I call the cell again and this time, leave a brief message for him to call me.

My mind on the woman next door, I give up on clearing my desk, turn off my computer, and hit the lights. But as I'm locking the door behind me, a police cruiser and an unmarked car pull in. I turn to face the parking lot and recognize Walker as he gets out of the car. From the look on his face I know he's here for me.

I wait for him to come up the steps, the officer right behind him.

"Please turn around, hands behind your back," he says, and I comply.

As the officer is snapping on the cuffs, my eyes meet Reagan's shocked ones through the door to her office.

"Callum McGregor, you are under arrest for the rape and sexual battery of Krista Hardee."

He grabs my elbow and turns me around. As I'm led down the steps I hear the door behind me open.

"Excuse me!" Reagan calls out, her voice strong and authoritative. "Where do you think you're going with my client?"

"Your client is under arrest," Walker fires off at her over his shoulder, as he presses me up against the cruiser.

Reagan hurries over as the officer pats me down, tossing my wallet, keys, and phone on the hood.

"Don't worry and don't say anything until I have a chance to find out what's going on," she urges me.

Not that I was planning to, but I can't deny I'm worried. I give her a nod and I get a reassuring smile in return. That settles my racing heart some.

"I'm good," I tell her, feeling far from it. "Can you take my phone and stuff? Call Mark?"

Mark is my second-in-command and I know from Moe he's around.

"For sure." She sounds calm but when she reaches to pick up my things, I see her hands shaking. She's not as composed as she appears. "I'm just gonna lock up and will be right behind you."

Her eyes hold mine as Walker puts me in the back of the cruiser, and they don't waver until we start moving.

Despite not having a clue what the fuck is going on, I trust Reagan enough to know she won't rest until she gets to the bottom of this.

CHAPTER SEVEN

Reagan

I'm vibrating with tension as I enter the police station.

A man I've seen go into McGregor Bail Bonds a few times gets up from a bench and walks toward me. He's tall, taller than Cal, fair-haired, clean-shaven, and well dressed. I already know he has a British accent.

"Mark?"

"Yes. Good to meet you," he returns with a nod.

"I'm surprised you got here this fast. Have you found out anything?"

He shakes his head. "Shaughnessy won't talk to me." He indicates the officer eyeing us from behind the desk. "You'll probably have more luck."

I nod and walk up to the counter.

"Officer Shaughnessy?"

"Sergeant Shaughnessy," he corrects me.

"I apologize, Sergeant. My name is Reagan Cole and I'm an attorney. I understand my client was arrested and brought in. Callum McGregor? I'd like to speak with him."

"Why don't you have a seat while I check with the arresting officer?"

"Could you perhaps tell me the exact charge?"

He looks at Mark over my shoulder, then seems to shrug.

"It's not a secret. Rape and sexual battery." He doesn't strike me as unfriendly so I reward him with a little smile.

"I see. One more question, if you don't mind?" I notice his eyes darting down the hallway, leading to the bowels of the building before returning to me. He leans a little closer.

"Be careful," he whispers under his breath just as Walker comes walking our way.

It takes everything out of me not to ask what he means, but the detective is watching us.

"Ms. Cole."

Oh, that man likes me about as much as I like him. Not.

"Detective Walker. I understand you've arrested my client."

"For a crime he committed, that's correct," he says smugly.

"I see you may need a refresher course in your criminal law, Detective. Guilt is decided in a court of law, by a jury of his peers, after hearing all the evidence. Which reminds me, I have left you several messages this past week, but you have failed to respond to any of them. Last time we spoke, you were going to check the cameras in the jail parking lot."

He throws a quick glance at Shaughnessy before returning to me.

"There's nothing worth seeing on the feed," he responds.

"Right. Could you see my client arrive?" I'm seething, but I'm trying to hold it together for my client.

"Possibly."

"What do you mean—possibly?"

"Couldn't really tell who it was, the tape was poor quality," he answers with a smug smile.

My hands are tight fists, nails digging into my palms, and I take a few deep breaths in.

"I will expect a copy of that tape."

"Sorry. I handed it over to the prosecutor's office. You'll have to get it from them."

"Do you at least have a copy of the warrant?"

"Shaughnessy can get that ready for you," he says magnanimously, and I'd love to plant my heel on his instep, but refrain.

"Good. Then I'd like a few minutes with my client now."

"I'm afraid he's being processed by the magistrate right now. You'll have to wait."

There isn't a doubt in my mind he'll keep me waiting longer than necessary, but there's little I can do about that, so I simply nod and walk over to Mark.

"I was wrong," he says when I take a seat on the bench beside him.

"Sorry?"

"When your brother first got in touch and told me to contact you, I wasn't sure it was a good idea. I'd seen you around and—please don't be offended—you didn't exactly have the appearance of an arse-kicker, but I stand corrected."

"Thanks—I think. Although I'm not so sure I've kicked any ass yet."

"Oh, but you will," he confirms with conviction.

I sure hope he's right, because there isn't a whole lot I can do for my client at this point.

"You know, you don't have to hang around," I tell Mark. "I'm sure it'll be a while before I get in to see him, and I can already tell you there's no way he'll get out today. We'll have to wait until Monday when he goes in front of a judge."

"I'm waiting with you."

Stubborn, but it's a free country and if he wants to sit on a bench in a police station on a weekend, I can't stop him.

At some point Shaughnessy walks up and hands me a copy of the arrest warrant, which I don't expect to offer anything I don't already know, but it gives me a chance to ask about his earlier warning.

"Why did you tell me to be careful?"

He throws a furtive glance over his shoulder before responding.

"Walker's an ass with connections, who somehow has developed a hard-on for your client. Don't know why, I just know he has the ear of the prosecutor's office."

"I see. Why are you telling me this?"

"Because I know and like McGregor, and this charge stinks to high heaven."

Someone walks in from outside and Shaughnessy rushes back to his post behind the desk and I turn to Mark.

"Have you guys had any run-ins with Detective Walker?"

"Not that I know of. I don't really know the guy. I can look into him if you like, though."

"Might be a good idea. At best, what they have on Cal is thin, hardly enough to be moving so fast on an arrest, so I'd love to know what Walker's beef is."

He gets to his feet. "I'll get on it right now. Will you be all right here? "

"I'll be fine. Thanks, Mark."

"Anything to get Cal out as soon as possible."

I just nod and watch him walk out the door.

As expected, it takes another hour and a half before an officer approaches and invites me to follow him to the holding cells.

I sit down on the cot beside Cal, who looks royally pissed.

"This is bullshit," he volunteers.

"I know." I lean in a little close to avoid being overheard. "Have you ever had a confrontation of some kind with Walker?"

The puzzled look on his face tells me enough.

"Didn't know the man before he walked into the interrogation room the first time. Why?"

"Remember I mentioned I thought he had his own agenda? I just had an interesting tête-à-tête with Shaughnessy in the lobby. He said to be careful of Walker, that he has connections, and something stinks about these charges."

He snorts. "No shit. They're bogus."

"Mark was here earlier, he's digging into Walker. I'm gonna look into that security feed, because something's fishy about that as well." I twist my body so I'm facing him. "The earliest I can get you out is Monday."

"I know. The magistrate can't allow bond on a violent felony charge."

Of course he would know.

"Exactly. Your case will go up in front of a judge for arraignment and I likely won't have a chance to talk to you before. You'll be asked to plea—"

"I'm familiar with the process," he interrupts brusquely.

"I'm sure you are, but I still need to go over this with you," I tell him firmly, before walking him through what to expect. More so for my sake, so I don't miss anything. "Can Mark access funds?"

"Yes."

"Okay, I'll ask him to be there with a check for your bail on Monday. We'll get this sorted."

I get up and tug my bag over my shoulder. His eyes drop to my mouth and I automatically lick them. His nostrils flare.

"Stop," I whisper.

"What am I doing?" he asks, an eyebrow raised.

"I'm your lawyer."

"I'm well aware."

"If you want me to continue representing you, you can't look at me like that. Especially in court."

"So noted."

Yet his gaze still burns me as the officer opens the door for me.

———

CAL

That was not pleasant.

I'm not talking about jail; that was luxurious compared to some places I've stayed in. No, what was hard to take was not being able to get myself out of this. I spent forty-eight hours fucking twiddling my thumbs while I had to trust others to do what needed to be done to get me out of here.

I'm not a stranger in the courtroom but I've never seen it from this perspective, which is something I could've done without. At first all I felt was anger that Krista would stoop this low, but now I'm starting to worry that even when I'm cleared, this will leave a lasting tarnish on my reputation.

"Pretrial is set for a week from today. I expect you there, Mr. McGregor."

Reagan elbows me and I reluctantly answer, "Yes, Your Honor."

After that it's a matter of Mark paying the bond and the three of us walk out of the courthouse.

"What the hell was with that prosecutor?" Mark asks Reagan.

A sour-faced lawyer from the Commonwealth's Attorney's Office entered a motion to deny me bail, but luckily the judge agreed with Reagan, who was prepared and calmly listed all the reasons I would not pose a flight risk.

"Not sure," she answers tensely, "but you can be assured I plan to find out."

She and Mark are parked side by side, but I opt to fold myself into the Kia's passenger seat. I'll catch Mark at the office but I want to talk to Reagan first.

"Talk to me," I tell her when she starts driving.

"There's a lot. Don't you want to go home first? Shower?"

I didn't think of that. I'm probably ripe by now.

"Fine. I'm not far. Familiar with The Lofts on East Washington?"

"I am."

"So fill me in?" I ask when she pulls onto the road.

"Don't hold your breath," she warns me with a quick side-glance. "There isn't a whole lot to tell you. At least on my side. I'm starting to suspect there was a purpose to arresting you on a

Saturday morning. I've still not had a call back from the Commonwealth's Attorney's Office, but I plan to park on their doorstep later today until I can get some answers."

When we stop at a traffic light, she presses her hand against her forehead and I notice for the first time how tired she looks.

"Are you okay?" My question seems to startle her.

The light turns green and it takes her a moment before she answers.

"Yeah, I'm good. I'm just frustrated. It feels like we're being railroaded. I haven't had a chance to confer with Mark yet, but I haven't been able to get anywhere."

I point her to my parking spot in front of my building and she follows me inside, not shy about checking out my place.

"Nice," she comments. "My real estate agent had me look at a show model for one of these lofts when I first moved here. The building was still being renovated then. Yours is nicer, though."

"Thanks. Look, make yourself comfortable. Feel free to help yourself to some coffee or something." I point at the kitchen. "I'll just be a few minutes."

It ends up being more like ten. As I wash the imaginary stench of the holding cell off me, I'm well aware of Reagan just feet away in my apartment and my body immediately responds. That eats up another few minutes to take care of. By the time I'm dressed and walk into the kitchen, she's sitting at the island, flipping through an old newspaper and sipping coffee. Fuck, but I like her in my space.

She turns when she hears me approach.

"Made you a cup too—"

Her words are cut off when I fist my hand in her hair and tilt her head back, my mouth kissing her hard. I don't miss her soft groan when I release her, or the flush on her cheeks, but still her eyes are guarded.

"Cal, we can't."

"Sweetheart, we just did." I reach around her for the coffee she set out for me and take a sip.

"No. I mean we *can't*. You're my client."

I set my coffee down and cup her face in my hands.

"And you're Muff's little sister, but that doesn't seem to deter me from wanting you. Tell me you don't feel the same way."

I hold her eyes, daring her to lie to me. She opens her mouth before closing it with a snap.

"Doesn't make a difference," she mumbles.

"That's where you're wrong, Reagan. It makes all the difference."

Before she has a chance to think, I fit my mouth over hers again. It doesn't take long for her fingers to curl into my shirt and I execute a mental fist pump.

CHAPTER EIGHT

Reagan

I've lost my ever-loving mind.

Stopping at a traffic light, I check my rearview mirror to see if Cal's truck is actually behind me. *Dammit.* I quickly pull up his number and dial just as the light turns green.

"What are you doing?" I snap the moment the call is answered.

"I told you; following you home."

"Cal..."

"You said we'd talk, so we'll talk when we get to your place."

"We can talk over the phone."

"Watch it!"

I'm so distracted watching him in my rearview mirror; I don't see the deer darting into the road in front of me until Cal yells out. Slamming on my brakes, I throw my wheel into the oncoming lane to avoid hitting it. Narrowly veering around the animal, I quickly check my mirror to see Cal's truck almost on top of me.

"Hang up the fucking phone before you kill yourself," he growls before ending the call.

My heart is racing as I focus on the road ahead.

It's my own fault; in an effort to get some control over a situation that seemed to be getting out of hand back in his apartment, I'd promised him we'd talk after meeting with Mark, who was waiting for us.

Mark had been at my office when we got there, chatting up Sally while he waited. She went off to put on a fresh pot while I hustled the guys into the conference room, where Mark filled us in on what he had been able to find out about Walker.

Apparently the detective joined the Suffolk PD, transferring from Norfolk just a couple of years ago. No blips on his record, not married, no kids. He rents a house in a new subdivision and seems to pay his bills on time. The only thing that piques any interest is his membership at a local gym. Mark offers to poke around there to see if he can stir anything loose.

Nothing to explain his apparent dislike of Cal.

We'd gone over the police report I was handed this morning. Krista Hardee's claim was ambiguous at best. Full of holes, incomplete, vague, and should never have even made it to an actual arrest without much more investigating. For one, she described a bed in the alleged assault, and then farther down her statement refers to the back seat of his vehicle. The other strange thing was the jail parking lot was not mentioned as the location where this attack was supposed to have taken place until the very last paragraph. To top it off, it looked like the statement was signed the same day Cal was first brought in for questioning, three days after it allegedly took place.

And the kicker? Walker's name was on the report.

While Cal went to try and get a hold of Jim Shaughnessy and see if he could convince the man to tell him what he knows, and Mark disappeared next door with him, I put another call into the prosecutor's office, this time asking for Ed Shafer's extension. He'd been the prosecuting attorney in court this morning. We've been opposing counsel a few times before and until this morning—when he completely ignored me—have always been friendly and courteous. His assistant told me he'd be held up in court this afternoon but I could leave him a message, which I did.

When I finally locked the office behind me—bone-tired and frustrated—I was startled by Cal's voice behind me.

"Heading home?"

I'm not sure if it was because he scared me senseless or whether senseless seems to be the way I am around him, but I nodded wordlessly. Then he told me he'd be following me home.

Checking the rearview mirror, I see he's pulling into my driveway behind me.

Well, I guess later is now but I have a suspicion talking is no longer first and foremost on Cal's mind.

I almost jog to my front door, the flock of butterflies back and swirling in my stomach. All I promised was a talk, but watching him approach with angry determination; he doesn't look like he's planning to waste any words.

He stays silent until I have the door unlocked and he follows me inside.

"You could've killed yourself. Fuck, if my brakes weren't brand-new, I coulda killed you."

I can tell he's pissed and even though I know he's right, my own temper flares and I immediately become defensive.

"Maybe if you hadn't been on my ass, following me home," I challenge, meeting his dark eyes shooting fire.

"You're telling me almost hitting that goddamn deer was my fault?"

"If the shoe fits," I return, shrugging as I turn toward the living room.

Next thing I know, I'm swung around and pressed with my back against the wall by Cal's big body. His face is inches away and he's breathing as hard as I am.

"Stop me," he says in a low voice.

But instead I lift my face and fist my hands in his shirt.

———

CAL

Christ, she makes my blood boil.

The kiss is angry—wild—driven by a hunger I can't seem to control, but I'm not alone. Reagan gives as good as she gets, her hands tugging the shirt from my jeans before shoving one of them up my back, her nails raking. Fuck me.

I slide my hands down to her ass, squeezing the luscious swells before I run one down to hitch her leg up. She moans into my mouth when I rock my hips between her opened legs, and starts pulling up my shirt. I need her out of these clothes and horizontal.

"Bedroom," I mumble against her lips, while my free hand slides up to cup her breast. No more than a perfect handful. She's killing me when she arches her back, her touch restless over my bared skin.

It's when she reaches for the waistband of my jeans I pull back and look into her heavy-lidded hazel eyes.

"Bed, Reagan."

She grabs my hand and pulls me to the stairs.

By the time she falls back on her bed, all she's left wearing is the pencil skirt she had on when she walked into court this morning—enhancing her generous curves—and nothing else. She's gorgeous; her hair loose and fanned out around her flushed face. I strip out of my clothes, even as my eyes trace her body; soft pale skin and deep pink nipples I can't wait to taste.

She's a fantasy, the perfect balance of classy and carefree.

From my jeans pocket I pull a condom I tucked there before I left the office, and roll it over my hard shaft. Then I grab her ankles, yank her closer to the edge, and run my hands up her legs, taking her skirt along.

"What are you doing?" She lifts up on her elbows, watching me.

Instead of answering, I hook my fingers in her panties and pull them off, leaving the bunched up skirt in place. Then I spread her legs, rub the head of my cock along her crease, slick with her arousal, and brace myself at her entrance.

With my last ounce of restraint, I lift my eyes and watch hers darken.

"*Please*," falls from her mouth as she lies back down.

Part of me is aware I'm not doing her any justice but I plan to make up for that later. An army wouldn't be able to stop me from driving myself balls deep in her tight channel.

"What time is it?"

Reagan lifts her head from my chest to glance at her alarm clock on the nightstand.

From the waning light through the window, I'm guessing around eight thirty or so, which would mean we've spent over three hours in this bed, and if it were up to me, we wouldn't leave it any time soon. I just need a little recovery time, at forty-five I don't bounce back the way I used to.

The first round was chaotic and wild and over way too soon, but the second time I made sure I took my time to familiarize myself with her body.

It's been a very long time since I've been in the mood for anything other than what is needed for a quick release. Don't really like what that says about me, but it's true. With Reagan, though, I could spend days leisurely exploring her body and discovering all the ways to make her moan.

"We should eat something. I'm hungry, aren't you?" she asks, as she slides out of my hold.

I catch her just around her middle as she swings her legs over the side and sits up, and I press my lips to the small of her back. She gives a little shiver and hugs my arm to her front, so I kiss her there again.

"Callum..."

"Yes, Sweetheart," I mumble, my lips against her skin.

"We need food...and then we still need to talk."

That gets my attention. We do need to talk—and to be honest—I could eat something.

I reluctantly let her go and watch her bare ass as she walks into the bathroom. And a spectacular ass it is.

I'm tempted to join her when I hear the shower turn on, but maybe she needs some time to get a handle on her thoughts. I know I do. I lie back, my arms folded under my head, and look up at the ceiling.

We've certainly broken some boundaries tonight there won't be any turning back from, but I can't bring myself to regret one single second of it. I don't want Reagan to either, so we'll need to do some damage control. First and foremost I need to talk to Muff, but I still haven't heard from him.

As if conjured, the sound of my phone ringing has me scramble off the bed to get it from my jeans.

"Finally," I answer, dropping back on the bed.

"Yeah, sorry," Jackson answers "Catherine and I needed some time away. We're in Costa Rica for a five-day break."

"Is everything okay?"

"Oh yeah. Life's just been busy. Anyway, I'm sorry I missed your calls, I haven't touched my phone in days."

"That's a good sign. Means you're actually relaxing."

He chuckles. "You can say that again."

"Cal? Was that mine?" My head swings around to see the bathroom door open and Reagan poking her head out, dripping water. "I thought I left it downstairs. Oops, sorry," she mutters when she sees me with the phone to my ear and promptly disappears again.

A heavy silence stretches on the other end of the call. I know he heard her.

"Yeah, so—"

"Was that my sister?" he interrupts sharply.

"It was."

Another pregnant pause.

"Please God, tell me I didn't catch you in bed with my sister."

When I don't answer immediately he lets out a string of creative curses.

"Technically, no," I clarify when he takes a breath. "She's in the shower and it's just me in bed."

I hold the phone away from my ear while he sets off swearing again.

"That's what you were calling about," he concludes once he runs out of steam.

"Look, I know this is breaking all the rules, but I really like her."

"I fucking hope so," he snaps.

"I was going to talk to you beforehand, but things got out of—"

"Yeah, thanks," he interrupts, "I get the picture."

"I'm sure you're pissed."

"You're fucking right I'm pissed. I mean I can't think of a better man for Reagan than you, but sonofabitch, couldn't you have held off? Do you know what this could do to her reputation? You're her client for fuck's sake."

I don't even register the rest of what he's saying; I'm stunned.

"You can't think of a better man for her?"

"Is there an echo in here or something? Of course, you idiot. You think I'd ask just anyone to look out for my sister? My point is you should've waited for this mess you're in to get cleared up."

"Right," I mumble, trying to wrap my head around this unexpected twist.

"And if you hurt her in any way, I will personally rip off your balls and shove them down your throat."

"So noted."

"Good. Now that we have that cleared up, I'd like to get back to my wife, who left for the beach ten minutes ago wearing the smallest fucking bikini I've ever seen," he grumbles.

"By all means."

His, "Fucking great," is followed by dead air.

When the bathroom door opens a few minutes later I'm still lying in bed, wondering what the hell just happened.

"Cal? Are you okay?"

I feel the mattress depress when Reagan sits down on the edge.

"Yeah." Even to my own ears I don't sound convincing.

"Who was on the phone?"

I scissor up and take her face in my hands, pressing a soft kiss on her mouth before looking deep into her eyes.

"Your brother."

I can pinpoint the exact moment the implications sink in.

"Oh, shit." She grabs onto my wrists. "That's not good."

"Actually..." I smile at her. "I think he may have just given us his blessing."

CHAPTER NINE

Reagan

"The door wasn't locked though."

I curb the urge to bang my head on my desk and take a few deep breaths instead. A sound from peanut gallery, aka Sally, has me throw her a sharp look to silence her.

The young kid in front of me is already defensive as all get out, even though he was caught street racing in a stolen Mercedes SUV. Not only that, a pedestrian was injured as a result and faces a long recovery.

Unfortunately, Emmet Licker—I still internally giggle like a five-year-old at that name—can't seem to focus on anything else but the fact the owner of the SUV had not locked the driver's side door. Apparently in Mr. Licker's world that is akin to finding a penny in a parking lot.

I've been trying to convince my client that accepting the plea deal the prosecution has offered will have the best outcome for him, but he still seems convinced that he was entirely within his rights. You can't argue stupid and unfortunately my client is severely afflicted.

"Forget about the SUV for a minute, Emmet," I try again. "Let's pretend you were driving your own car."

"I don't got a car, I drive my Pops's truck."

"Fine," I conceded. "Let's pretend you were driving the truck, and were street racing, and hit another person. You would still be breaking the law."

"That's just dumb." He folds his arms over his skinny chest and pouts like a toddler.

"Listen, I can't tell you what to do, I can only advise you, but I can promise two years plus probation is the absolute best you can do. All you have to do is plead guilty in front of the judge."

"Pops said you could get me off," he insists, this twenty-three-year-old boy-child.

'Pops' is Darren Licker, owner of a farm equipment dealership just outside of town. Clearly the one with all the brains of the family, although, he's lacking in parental skills and spoils his only son rotten.

"Your father hired me because I'm very good at what I do, which is why you should take my advice." We've been around and around on this, and it doesn't look like what I'm saying is permeating. Perhaps I should give Darren a call. "You know what?" I tell the kid. "Why don't you go home, think about it tonight, talk to your father, and get back to me tomorrow? We have to give them an answer before the weekend."

"Fine."

I can't hold back the roll of my eyes when he gets up and heads for the door, the crotch of his jeans around his knees making for an awkward gait. The moment the front door shuts behind him, Sally bursts out giggling and I'm not far behind.

"You have permission to put me out of my misery and shoot me if Matt should end up like that waste of space."

We're still snickering five minutes later when the door opens and Cal walks in. Immediately my cheeks flush, remembering our activities from last night. Activities that left me deliciously sore in places.

He's been by my house every night so far this week. Three nights in a row we've ended up naked, and three times he's left me well sated in my bed to go home. I haven't asked him to stay, and he hasn't offered. Don't get me wrong, at some point I'd love for him to spend the night, but for now I'm grateful for my rest after he leaves.

There is also the fact I'd rather whatever we have going on does not go public. At least not yet. Not until we have the case against him dismissed.

"Hey, you left a message for me?" he asks, after saying hello to Sally.

"Yes, I told you I stopped at the prosecutor's office on Tuesday and was able to talk to Ed Shafer. Well, he emailed me this morning with the surveillance tape. I wanted to wait for you before I had a look at it." He moves to sit down across from me when I hold up my hand and push back my chair. "Let's take it into the conference room," I suggest, leading the way.

We've barely crossed the threshold when I feel his heat at my back and am just able to set my laptop on the table when I'm swung around.

"Morning, Sweetheart," he rumbles, a fraction of a second before he takes my mouth in a claiming kiss that leaves me gasping for air.

"Boundaries," I whisper, but not before licking my bottom lip where his taste lingers.

"Right," he confirms, but with a wink. "Before we look at that," he points at the computer, "I should tell you I bumped into Jim Shaughnessy at the Main Street Diner this morning."

"Bumped into him?" I raise an eyebrow, knowing that he's been trying to pin the man down for a few days now.

"Fine, I cornered him in a booth," he admits with a lopsided grin. "He wasn't too pleased to see me and he really didn't like when I sat down across from him. There were a couple of other cops sitting at the counter he was keeping an eye on, but he did talk. Said he was warning you because Walker has it in for me."

"But why?"

I sit down in a chair and look up at him as he sits down on the edge of the table.

"Get this; Shaughnessy says Walker had been seeing Krista."

"Well, isn't that an interesting twist? So what? He's pissed that you brought her back?" I wonder out loud.

"Not a clue, but Mark is already digging into it. He's good digging up all kinds of shit on the computer, he'll find out."

I look at him sternly. "If you're talking about hacking into stuff without a warrant, I don't wanna know about it," I warn him, and he grins.

"Then I won't tell you."

———

CAL

"See that lamppost on the far side of the parking lot?"

I point at the screen and Reagan leans in close, squinting her eyes.

This is the worst quality surveillance footage I've ever seen. I can barely recognize myself. Of course, I'm only shown from behind and some of it looks pretty damning. You can see me ducking into the back seat and wrestling with someone. Damn Krista, she scooted all the way to the far side when I opened her door and started kicking at me. She fought me the whole time I tried to get her out of the truck and finally bit me. I should've pressed charges on *her*.

"What am I looking at?"

"See that box about two-thirds up that post? That's another camera. Mark checked it out, he says there are at least three cameras aimed at that side of the parking lot."

"Then where are the tapes for those cameras?"

"Fuck if I know, but I sure would like to."

"Hang on one sec," Reagan says, darting out the door.

A minute later she comes walking in with a phone to her ear.

"Extension 213, please."

I listen in as she—unsuccessfully—attempts to get hold of Ed Shafer.

"No luck," I offer when she tosses her phone on the table with a frustrated growl.

"He's not available," she grinds out. "We're being stonewalled. No way we'll hear anything before the pretrial hearing on Monday."

"I don't get their issue with me, though," I contemplate. "I'd never seen Shafer before the arraignment. Even if Shaughnessy is right, and Walker has it in for me, it doesn't explain why the prosecutor's office is so determined to see me go down."

Reagan shakes her head before getting up and grabbing her things off the table.

"You busy right now?"

"Nothing that can't wait. Why?" I ask.

"Because when we walk into court on Monday, I want to be able to at least discredit any evidence the prosecutor produces."

I follow her to her desk where she stuffs her laptop and a notepad in her briefcase.

"Sally?" The woman turns to Reagan. "Where is that digital camera we used in the Collins case?"

"Bottom drawer of the small filing cabinet."

"What are we doing?" I ask, enjoying the view as Reagan bends over in yet another tight pencil skirt. Her assistant catches me watching and snickers openly.

"We are going to collect some evidence of our own to at least discredit what the prosecution brings to the table." She turns to Sally holding up a nice-looking Nikon camera. "Is this charged?"

"There's an extra lithium battery pack in the bag."

"You know you can take pictures with your cell phone, right?" I suggest.

"Snapshots, yes, but this baby date-stamps everything, has a powerful zoom, and gives me raw image files I can hand over to the judge on an SD card. Harder to tamper with and therefore much more reliable in terms of evidence."

I grin at her. It's kind of a turn-on to see her in action.

"I'm gone for the afternoon, Sally. Call me if anything urgent comes up."

"Will do."

I tip my imaginary hat at Sally as I follow Reagan out the door.

"Can we take your truck?"

"Sure." I would've suggested it myself since I don't feel like folding up like an origami crane to get into her toy car, but this works even better. "Let me grab my keys and tell Pooja I'm off."

When I come back outside, Reagan is already waiting by the passenger side door.

"I take it we're heading to the jail parking lot?" I guess when I back out of my parking spot.

She looks at me and smiles big.

"That's the plan."

She has me park the truck in the same spot in front of the jail I stopped at the night I dropped off Krista. Then she proceeds to take stills and footage of the cameras I point out, and has me reenact my movements from that night. When a security guard comes out demanding to know what we're doing, she sweet-talks him and gets him to confirm he could see us on all three camera feeds.

She's masterful, using her looks and her charm to hide her cunning intelligence and disarm the man into that admission. He doesn't even look at me twice.

I'm grinning when I settle behind the wheel, watching Reagan buckle up.

"What?"

"You. I knew you were smart, but I had no idea how slick you could be."

She shrugs her shoulders and presses her lips together to hide a smile.

"Part of the job."

"Well, color me impressed. It's hot as fuck seeing you in action."

I like seeing the familiar blush rising to her cheeks. It doesn't seem to matter I had her riding my face last night—dirty talk softly flowing from those kissable lips as she ground herself down to completion with abandon—she still responds like an innocent and I love that about her.

"Whatever," she mumbles, turning her gaze out the window.

"Where to next?"

"Let's go find Oliver Hardee."

I snap my head around. "Krista's father?"

"Yup. Let's see what—if anything—he knows about Walker."

"I'm not so sure you're gonna want me there," I suggest. "Given I'm accused of sexually assaulting his daughter, he may not react too favorably to talking."

"On the contrary," she disagrees, throwing a sly smile my way. "If I try to approach him by myself, he'll likely brush me off. If he's any kind of father, however, the sight of you will infuriate him. An angry man rarely uses discretion and won't think about what he should or shouldn't be saying."

I'm pretty sure my mouth is hanging half open as I look over at her.

"Remind me never to get on the other side of a courtroom from you."

———

We finally caught up with the real estate mogul on the tenth hole at the golf course. It wasn't a surprise to see a couple of councilmen as part of his foursome. He's been known to wheel and deal permits and apparently isn't shy about it.

The moment he recognized me walking up behind Reagan, he reacted much as she had predicted. He marched toward us and his entire focus was on me, throwing accusations and barely noticing Reagan. She was able to interject some pointed questions, which he almost distractedly responded to before tearing back into me.

By the end of it, I'd been used as a verbal punching bag, Reagan had needed to step in a time or two to keep fists from flying, but when we drove off we had the confirmation we were looking for. Not only that, but Hardee volunteered Walker had promised him he had connections in the prosecutor's office and could make sure the charges would stick.

"Listen to this."

We've just pulled up to Joe's for a quick bite when Reagan produced her cell phone.

"What am I listening to?"

Instead of answering, she plays me recordings she apparently made of not only Hardee, but the security guard as well.

"Holy shit. Those may not stand, though, you didn't have consent," I point out as I get out of the truck.

"I won't need it," she says when I open the door for her. "In Virginia only one party to a conversation needs to consent for it to be a legal recording." She grins at me widely. "And I consent."

I shake my head and smile back. "I'm firing Milt."

"Who's Milt?"

"Milt Arenberg, my soon-to-be former legal representation. I want you on retainer."

She laughs and I follow her to the entrance to the restaurant when the phone in her hand starts ringing.

"Sally, what's up?"

She abruptly stops and I can see shock replace the smile she was sporting.

"What do you mean there's a fire?"

CHAPTER TEN

Reagan

My heart is in my throat as Cal races toward the office.

My God, my office, all my case files.

I'm desperately trying to remember how long ago it was I asked Sally to upload all digital copies to the cloud.

Sally. Oh my God, I didn't even ask her if she was okay. I'd called her earlier to let her know I was going to grab a bite and wouldn't be back until later. When I told her I needed to draw up a few motions for Monday, she offered to stay since Matt is with his father this weekend.

I can see the dark smoke curling up when we're still a few blocks away, and fire trucks are already in front of the building by the time we pull up along the curb. We can't get in the parking lot, which is blocked off by police cruisers on either side.

The moment the truck stops rolling I have the door open. Ignoring Cal's, "Hold up," I hop down and start jogging toward the office, hearing him curse behind me.

"Ma'am."

I try to get by the young officer when I spot Sally sitting on the bumper of my Kia Soul with another cop crouching in front of her, but I'm hauled back with an arm around my middle. My legs turn to rubber.

"Easy, Slick, let's find out what's going on first."

Cal pulls me in front of him, holding me firm around the waist and bracing the other one in across my chest as he turns us toward the officer.

"That's my building," he explains to the younger man. "I'm the McGregor of McGregor Bail and Bonds, and Reagan here owns Cole law offices. Sally over there is her paralegal." He tilts his chin in the direction of my assistant. "What happened?"

"We're trying to find that out, sir. The garbage bin was rolled up against the rear entrance and it appears the fire originated there."

"Arson," I bite off, my eyes fixed on the orange glow I can see through the front window of my office.

"That's for the fire inspector to confirm, ma'am, but unless that dumpster is usually parked against the back door, I would say it sure looks like it."

"It's not," Cal confirms.

A car door slams and I turn my head to see Mark jogging up.

"What the fuck? I just left half an hour ago to grab some food," he mumbles in passing, ignoring the protests of the police officer as he makes his way over to Sally.

An hour and a half later, the four of us are sitting on the curb, waiting for the fire inspector to finish his walk-through with a detective from the SPD. Not Walker, but an older man who was known to Cal and Mark.

The fire is out, and although it looks like most of the fire was to the back of the building, smoke and water damage is extensive. I'll be surprised if we can salvage anything usable but we aren't allowed in until the fire inspector is done.

Cal already called the insurance company and I have a separate tenants' policy, which covers everything inside my walls through the same place. He says we should be covered and I hope he's right, but furniture is the least of my worries. There's also the matter of my slashed tires.

Mark was the one who noticed when he walked up to join

Sally. I guess when a building is on fire it draws the focus. So yeah, all four tires, which of course begs the question, why would someone set the office on fire *and* slash the tires on my car. You'd think just one of those would be enough to send a message if that was the intent.

I noticed Cal and Mark exchanging looks I can't quite decipher, and to be honest, I'm reeling too hard to pay more than a passing attention to it. Sally's hand is clasped in mine and I'm beyond grateful she wasn't injured.

She'd been in the kitchen, doing some dishes and making a pot of coffee while listening to her audio book. She can't recall hearing anything—she was wearing earbuds—but remembers noticing the smell of smoke at some point. When the alarm started blaring, she immediately called 9-1-1 and made her way outside, where a passing patrol car had already noticed the smoke and was pulling in.

All four of us rush to our feet when the two investigators come walking out of the building.

"Mr. McGregor?"

"That's me," Cal volunteers. "And this is Reagan Cole, my tenant."

The rotund fire inspector gives me a nod before focusing on him.

"Definitely arson. The dumpster was rolled up to the back door, blocking it and both the door and the bin look to have been doused in an accelerant. As far as arsons go, it was a half-assed attempt. The bulk of the damage is to the back of the building, impacting the smaller of the two units. The roof in the rear was involved and sustained substantial damage."

"I don't think the fire was necessary the ultimate objective," the police detective suggests.

"What do you mean?" I ask.

"Well, as I understand it the Kia with the slashed tires is yours, correct?"

"It is."

He flips through a small notebook before he adds, "But you were out with Mr. McGregor in his vehicle."

"Correct. I'm not sure—"

"Bear with me please?" he asks with a kind smile. "Was your car in this condition when you left with Mr. McGregor?"

I try to think back whether I noticed anything off. I didn't, but I couldn't swear to it.

"It wasn't," Cal answers for me. "I would've noticed."

"Right. So unless you have two separate individuals who mean to get your attention at the very same time, I would say it's safe to assume both the tires and the fire are at the same hands. Which..." he quickly adds when I open my mouth, "...leads me to conclude someone is not happy with you."

"Why both, though?" Sally pipes up. "I mean why bother with the tires? Unless..."

"Ms. Cole," the detective draws my attention. "Can you think of anyone who is angry with you?"

I can't help it, I snort.

"Look, Detective..."

"Melville."

"Detective Melville, I'm a criminal defense lawyer, having people upset with me comes with the territory. Besides, I wasn't even here," I offer, but my mind is already going over a list of possible suspects.

"But your car was. The blinds were closed but the light was on. Someone might've concluded you were," he counters. "Ms. Cole, I'd like you to make a list of people who might be unhappy with you as soon as possible, and call me so we can go over it." He hands me a card he fishes from his pocket.

"Can we go in?" Cal asks. "Collect equipment and files we can salvage?"

"We're done in there, but you may want to check with your insurance adjuster first."

We watch the men walk toward their respective vehicles and drive off. Then it's just us outside the building.

"Let's do this," Mark suggests.

I nod but I have to force my feet to start moving. I'd rather have a root canal without freezing than go in there and face the destruction of my office, but I don't really have a choice.

Halfway to the front door I feel a hand grabbing mine, giving it a reassuring squeeze.

It helps.

———

CAL

The moment we step in the door at Reagan's, she turns and does a face plant in my chest. My arms circle her instinctively.

"You okay, Sweetheart?"

I feel her shake her head against me and I bury my nose in her hair. She smells of smoke, like I'm sure I do too.

We just spent a few hours grabbing anything worth rescuing and piled it in both my truck and Mark's. My side of the building had little fire damage—only part of the ceiling in the back—but water and smoke damage was substantial. Nothing like Reagan's side, though. That looked pretty bad. I'm going to meet with the insurance adjuster tomorrow morning but even if he cuts me a check right there and then, it'll take weeks if not months to make the repairs necessary.

Moe showed up before we left and was going to help Mark make sure the place will be as secure as possible overnight. Mark was first going to see Sally home safe, and then they're taking what we pulled from the bail bonds office to my apartment downtown for the time being.

Reagan's stuff is in the back of my truck, I should get that inside somewhere in case it rains, but first I need to make sure she's okay.

"You reek of smoke," she mumbles against my shirt.

"I know. We both do. Let's get you cleaned up."

She leans back and looks at me. "What about you?"

"I'm first gonna get your stuff inside. Is your garage unlocked?"

"You can just bring it in here."

"I was actually just going to pull the truck into the garage so we can worry about it tomorrow."

"Right." She pulls from my arms and grabs her key ring from the hall table where she tossed them, selecting one. "This is the garage. You may have to move the lawnmower out of the way."

"I'll go take care of that while you hop in the shower."

She's staring unfocused somewhere over my shoulder.

"My car."

"We'll take care of that tomorrow as well."

Her eyes come to me, tears pooling.

"Sally?"

"Mark saw her home. She's good. We'll do damage control tomorrow."

"Right." She nods, but doesn't move.

I take her face in my hands and kiss her softly.

"Upstairs, Sweetheart. You're swaying on your feet."

I wait until she reaches the top of the stairs before I turn and head outside. It takes me a couple of minutes to make room in the garage and secure my truck. When I return to the house I can hear the shower running upstairs, but instead of heading up, I go in search of her laundry. All I have are the clothes on my back and they're rank, so I strip down and toss them in the washer.

The bathroom is steamed up but empty and I quickly hop in the shower myself, washing the smoke and the soot off.

Clean but tired, I wrap a towel around my hips and move into the bedroom, where Reagan's form is visible under the covers. I slide in beside her and she immediately turns toward me.

"Thank you," she mumbles drowsily. "I'm so tired, I don't know if I'm up—"

"Hush. Go to sleep." I press a kiss on her head and hold her close until I can feel her body relax and her breath even out.

I lie like that, with Reagan's naked skin pressed to me, and am surprised to find that despite the fact my body notices, the overwhelming feeling is the need to protect her.

Sleep doesn't come easy for me, my mind trying to make sense of the events of tonight and going into problem-solving mode. I make a mental list of things I have to take care of tomorrow, people I have to call to make sure my business can keep rolling. Pooja's first on my list, she can take care of most of it, so I can stick around here and give Reagan a hand.

I'm too wired and at some point, I untangle myself from Reagan and go downstairs to grab a drink. I flip on the TV and watch a twenty-four-hour news station while I wait for the washer to finish. Once my clothes are in the dryer, I head back up.

It looks like Reagan is still sleeping, but when I slide under the covers her eyes open a crack.

"I thought you'd left," she mumbles in a sleepy voice.

"Not a chance," I whisper back, tucking her close.

"Good. I want you to stay."

CHAPTER ELEVEN

Reagan

"Oh my God..."

I feel his responding chuckle through my body, his face buried in my neck and his cock deep inside me. He lifts up on an elbow and with his other hand brushes away strands of hair stuck to my damp forehead.

He looks good in the morning; a cocky smile behind his beard, eyelids still heavy with sleep, and his hair sticking out in every which way. The hair is mostly my doing, since I held on tight when I woke up with his mouth between my legs.

"Perks of staying the night," he mumbles, gently sliding in and out of me as we both recover slowly. "Been so long, I'd almost forgotten."

I try not to show how pleased I am with that admission. Silly, since it's not like either of us have been monks with half a life already behind us, but it still makes me feel good. Special, somehow.

"I liked you staying here," I make an admission of my own, my hands stroking his back. "Don't get me wrong, the sex is... whew, but..." I add quickly when I see his grin grow smug, "being able to fall asleep safely in someone's arms after a really shitty day felt amazing."

I wince a little when he pulls out, kissing me between my breasts as he slides off the bed.

"Yeah." His eyes are soft looking down on me. "Agreed on both counts."

He grabs my ankles and pulls my legs over the side.

"What are you doing?" I complain.

"Time to get up, Slick. I could stay in bed with you for the weekend and not come up for air, but it's almost eight and I'm pretty sure Sally will be knocking on the door shortly."

Right. This is not a casual Saturday morning.

I'm surprised to find him at the stove when I come downstairs. In the time it took me to dry my hair and slap on a little makeup, he's been busy.

"French toast?" I lean over and peek in the pan.

"Cream cheese and banana stuffed French toast, yes."

"My mouth is watering." I reach in the pan to pinch off a bite but he slaps my hand.

"Patience. It needs a few more minutes. Why don't you make yourself some coffee?"

As expected the food is delicious and I scarf it down. I'm about to complain about how full I am when a knock sounds at the front door.

"I'll get it," Cal says and gets up.

I start cleaning up when I hear him greet Sally and both of them walk into the kitchen.

"Morning. Get any sleep?"

I glance over at Cal, whose eyes are dancing.

"I did, surprisingly. What about you?" I ask Sally.

She shrugs and pulls out a stool at the island.

"Meh, so-so. That did leave me with lots of time to think of solutions to our current predicament. I also made a list of possible individuals who have a bone to pick with us."

I love that she uses the term 'us' instead of you. I feel guilty enough she could've gotten hurt.

"Perfect. Why don't I make you a coffee and we can go over your list?"

"Before you do that," Cal interrupts. "I'm going to get my truck and pull it up to your porch to start unloading it. Do you have any cleaner I can use? It'll all smell of smoke, so I'll try to clean what I can before bringing it inside."

"Laundry room."

I leave him to look while I work on coffee for Sally. An arm slips around my stomach and I feel his kiss on my exposed shoulder where my shirt has slipped down. I feel the flush rising to my cheeks, as it tends to do when he's around.

"Make me another one too?" he asks softly, before his heat disappears from behind me.

"Sure."

I hope my color is back to normal by the time I turn around to hand my assistant her cup. Sally's eyes twinkle and her smile is wide.

"I just want you to know I'm jealous as fuck and I'm pretty sure I hate you a little, but I can't deny you look good together. I like him for you."

I smile back. "Good. I like him for me too. Now, about that list."

"Well, you know I have your asshole ex at the top of it," she says unapologetically.

"I don't know if that's Neil's style, though, Sal. It seems a little too...I don't know...unsophisticated? I have no doubt he'd love to see me go under, although for the life of me I can't figure out why."

"That's easy," she says, surprising me. "He's always known you were the better lawyer, and he's crazy jealous you've successfully struck out on your own."

"Oh, I don't know. He's got a pretty good thing going as a prosecutor."

She snorts. "Please, he only got into the Richmond

Commonwealth's Attorney's Office because of his father. You talk about him like he was once some idyllic Robin Hood figure, working as a public defender before he lost his shine. Have you ever considered he was never that heroic?" She leans forward with her elbows on the counter. "I looked into his cases once. Did you know he won no more than a handful of cases before he joined his father's office? And the cases he won as a prosecutor were ones they could've put a baboon in charge of and it wouldn't have made a difference. They were slam-dunk cases.

"I'm sorry, I know you were married to the man, but he's a petty, little dipfuck and I wouldn't put anything past him."

That gives me a minute's thought. I wonder if she's right and it's just been easier to think he was once a good man turned asshole, rather than admit he was one all along and I may have been too young and too blind to see it.

"Who else do you have on your list?"

"Sean Davis," she answers right away.

"Sean? Why? I could see if I lost his case, but I didn't."

"No, but you did reject him."

"I'm not buying it. Who's next?"

"That creepy kid; Emmet Licker. He never called yesterday."

I'd completely forgotten about that. Shit, I'm supposed to let the prosecutor know if my client is taking the deal.

"Why would he try to burn down my office?"

"Because he doesn't wanna go to jail. He didn't seem too eager to accept the plea deal, and hearing you weren't going to magically make those charges disappear may have been a rude awakening for him. Maybe it was desperation, hoping somehow torching your office would make it all go away. Who knows? The kid's a limp noodle, he wears his goddamn pants around his knees."

"What's this about pants around his knees?" Cal asks, walking in.

"One of Reagan's clients."

"Oh?" Cal looks at me with his eyebrow raised. "Should I be worried?"

Sally snickers and I hand Cal his fresh coffee and reassure him with a smile.

"Not even a little."

CAL

"Pooj? Can you run up to MinuteKEY and get five extra copies made?"

I hand her the key to my apartment. I'll need one for her, three for the guys, and I want an extra one to give to Reagan, just in case.

I left both her and Sally to deal with what they needed to do after helping them rearrange Reagan's furniture in her home office. We were able to fit in Sally's desk—which we were able to salvage—as well as the two heavy filing cabinets. It's tight, but workable in a pinch. The few other pieces of furniture we were able to rescue we ended storing in the garage for now.

"Sure thing. Need me to pick up some lunch?"

"Chick-fil-A," Moe yells out from the kitchen, where he's quickly depleting the contents of my fridge.

"You haven't stopped eating yet!" Pooja yells back.

Since she's the one who will be in the office most, we put her desk in front of the window in the living room. The guys did a decent job last night, and early this morning, hauling almost the entire contents of our offices into my apartment. Luckily the loft is a decent size and other than the bathroom and my bedroom, an open concept. I had a pretty minimalistic decor, so other than moving my couch and easy chair out of the way, it wasn't too difficult to get a few desks in here.

"Those were snacks," Moe answers, still chewing as he walks up. "I need something substantial."

"Fine," I intervene, or these two would keep up their bickering forever. "Pooj, if you don't mind, take orders." I toss a few bills on her desk. "Lunch is on me today. And have you heard from Dean?"

"He called in yesterday afternoon, after you left. He's close, he expects to be back Tuesday or Wednesday."

Dean is the third bondsman on my team. There are four of us plus Pooja, who basically runs the office. Of the five on our team, she's the indispensable one. The rest of us rotate interchangeably through the cases, but she is our constant.

"What about you?"

"I had a big breakfast," I tell her. "Besides, I have to make tracks. I've got to meet up with the insurance adjuster."

"Oh, that reminds me, should I call Brand Automotive to tow Reagan's car while you're there?"

"Sure. I have a contractor coming to take a preliminary look too. May as well get as much done as I can while I'm there."

I leave her to get the orders from the guys and disappear into my bedroom to pack a bag. I haven't discussed in so many words whether Reagan would be agreeable to me bunking at her place for the time being, but this morning she seemed on board with the concept, which I'll gladly take as acceptance. The more important consideration is the possibility she's in danger. The setup yesterday—the fire and the disabling of her car—almost implies someone was trying to get her outside and vulnerable. It ended up not being Reagan in the office and luckily a police cruiser happened by, otherwise things might have turned out a little different.

It doesn't take me long to grab my stuff together. I'm tossing my shampoo and bodywash into my bag—as much as I love the scent of Reagan's soap on her, I don't so much on me—when Mark saunters into my bedroom.

"So it's like that," is his only comment when he sees me packing.

"It is." I zip the bag shut and sling it over my shoulder. "You've got an issue with that?"

He barks out a laugh. "Hell no, far from it. You're moving fast, that's all."

"Who are you? My mother?" I'm instantly annoyed.

His answer is a pair of defensive hands he holds up.

"Just looking out for you. She's your defense attorney."

I take in a calming breath before responding.

"I'm well aware. Look, I hear what you're saying, and I appreciate your concern, which is the only reason I'm even responding. If not for what happened yesterday, I might not have been packing my bag today, but I have no doubt it would've happened eventually."

"You feel that way about her?"

He seems incredulous which pisses me off, even though I know where he's coming from. I'm not one for relationships. I think the times any of my employees have seen me with a woman over the years can be counted on a sawyer's handful.

"Not that it's any of your fucking business, but yes. Now, can you step the fuck aside so I can get on my way?"

I ignore his grin as he moves to one side, letting me slip through.

———

Later that afternoon when I walk into Reagan's house with my bag, she and Sally are still working. Both heads come up and turn my way. Sally is smiling when she sees the large pizza box on top of the case of beer I'm carrying, but Reagan's eyes are focused on the bag over my shoulder before they meet mine.

"Not sure what your plans are, Sally, but I brought enough pizza for us all."

"No plans and I'm starving. If I wasn't afraid my boss might scratch my eyes out, I'd kiss you right now," she answers and I grin at her, but when I look at Reagan she's not smiling.

"What about you, Slick? Hungry?"

"Give us ten minutes?"

"You bet."

I dump my bag at the bottom of the stairs and take the pizza into the kitchen, where I grab three plates from the cupboard and tear off some paper towels. I shove the pizza box in the oven, hoping it'll stay warmer in there, and am stacking the fridge with beer when Reagan walks into the kitchen.

"Uh, Cal?"

I see the concern in her eyes, and respond by pulling her into my arms and covering her mouth with mine.

"Hi," I whisper when I come up for air, my nose touching hers. Her beautiful eyes blink at me, but the worry is still there. "My apartment is now my office, which has to house five people when we're all in town. You seemed happy I stayed the night, so I kinda assumed..."

She shakes her head sharply.

"That's not it. I just discovered something when you walked in."

She looks almost guilty.

"What is it?"

"I was catching up on emails and there was one from Shafer, the prosecutor. He apologized for not getting back to me on the tapes from the jail security, but said he had no access to them. Apparently he was only standing in for someone else from his office last Monday."

"So he's not the one handling my case?"

"No. Neil Tory is."

She looks at me like that name is supposed to mean something to me, but other than it sounds vaguely familiar, I can't place it.

"Should I know who that is?" I finally ask.

"I guess not, since he's a subject that hasn't come up yet. Neil Tory is my ex-husband."

Now I can place the name. I'm pretty sure Jackson

mentioned it at some point. I remember he didn't have much love for the man.

"I'm guessing that's not a good thing?"

She snorts nervously at that.

"No. I'm afraid he may be using your case for a chance to get back at me."

CHAPTER TWELVE

Reagan

I dig up the card Detective Melville handed me.

When Sally first mentioned putting Neil at the top of her list yesterday, I brushed it off as too farfetched. Now I'm not so sure. I also wouldn't have thought he'd ever pursue a case as questionable as the one against Cal, but he is and I can't help but think it's because of me.

Cal and I butted heads yesterday when I told him the best course of action all around would be for me to withdraw from his case. That went over like a lead balloon. When Sally came into the kitchen and squarely backed Cal on his insistence I stay on the case, agreeing with him that making any changes now would only cause a delay, I gave in. The truth is, it *would* cause a delay and I don't want Cal to have to walk around with this cloud over his head any longer than necessary.

"Melville."

"Detective Melville, it's Reagan Cole. I'm sorry to disturb you on a Sunday, but you asked me to let you know if I have a list of people who may not be too happy with me."

"In this line of work, the days of the week blend together," he says. "You were able to come up with some names?"

"With the help of my assistant, yes."

"Any chance you could meet me at the station before noon? I promised my wife I'd be home this afternoon, but a new case popped up overnight," he explains apologetically.

I glance at the clock. It's just shy of eleven and it'll only take me fifteen minutes to get downtown.

"I can. I'll see you shortly."

When I hang up, I find Cal leaning against the doorway to my office, a garment bag folded over an arm. He must've just walked in.

After pizza last night, Sally and I worked until about ten when she left. We wanted to get the motions done for Monday —Sally had things to do today—and had some trouble converting the voice recordings from my phone onto a USB-key. By the time I closed the door behind her, I found Cal had gone upstairs already. He was fast asleep in my bed.

This morning I found a note on the kitchen island from him. He'd already gone out to pick up the suit he'd forgotten at his place for court tomorrow. I'd expected him back a while ago but I guess he got hung up.

"That was Detective Melville," I volunteer, as I fold the list I printed off this morning and tuck it in my purse. "I'm supposed to meet him at the police station."

"Good. I'll be right down, I'm just going to hang this up."

He turns on his heel and I hear his heavy footfalls go up the stairs. It's strange, suddenly sharing my space with someone. I didn't object when he showed up with his stuff yesterday, mostly because what happened Friday night shook me to the core. On a rational level, I realize there's always a chance as a criminal lawyer you piss someone off, but it had always been more of an abstract concept. There was nothing abstract about what happened Friday, and having Cal stay here with me makes me feel safer.

By the time his footsteps come back down the stairs, I'm waiting by the front door. He walks straight up to me and takes my face in his hands.

"Forgot something," he mumbles, right before he covers my mouth with his, kissing me sweetly. "Morning."

"Morning to you." I smile up at him, running my fingers along the short hairs of his trimmed beard. "You don't have to come with me, you know."

He cracks a grin. "No? How do you propose to get there with your car in the shop?"

Shit. I'd forgotten my car was towed, making me effectively dependent on Cal and his wheels.

"Forgot."

"I figured."

He slides a hand down my arm and slips his fingers between mine before pulling the door open.

"Did they say when my car would be ready?" I ask when we get on the road.

"He said he'd be able to drop it off when it's done, probably Tuesday afternoon. Which reminds me, your insurance company will want a copy of the police report, both for the office and your car."

"Right." I'll have to see whether it's worth paying the deductible on my car insurance, or just pay for new tires out of pocket.

"By the way, I was also gonna talk to you about the contractor. As soon as I hear back from the adjuster, he'll be able to get construction started within a day or two. Ballpark, he expects it to take around a month."

A heavy sigh escapes me and Cal immediately glances over.

"It's fine," I quickly assure him. "It just means I'm back to meeting clients in public places. I don't want to invite them into my house. It's what I used to do before I started renting from you."

"Probably smart."

"I should also give Jackson a call. Get him up-to-date."

My brother is the protective kind, and he wouldn't be too

pleased if he found out about what happened in some round-about way.

"Talked to him this morning."

I snap my head around, glaring at him.

"I would've liked to have told him myself."

"Didn't call him, Slick, he called me. It was about something unrelated, but he asked how things were with you and I wasn't gonna lie."

As much as I wanted to talk to him myself, I appreciate Cal has his own relationship with Jackson. One that apparently requires honesty. Another mark on the plus side. Apparently my brother trusts him or he would've been on the phone with me right after.

"Do I have to worry he's gonna show up on my doorstep heavily armed?"

It suddenly occurs to me that's a distinct possibility. Cal's easy chuckle fills the cab of the truck.

"I don't think so, but he did demand daily briefings."

I roll my eyes. He would too.

CAL

Detective Melville shows us into an empty office.

"Have a seat."

I wait for Reagan to sit before I follow suit. The detective sits across from us and gets straight to the point.

"You have a list for me?"

Reagan digs in her purse and hands over a folded sheet of paper. Melville takes a perfunctory first glance before I see his eyebrows pull together sharply. He looks up at Reagan and then back down on the page.

"You have an officer of the Commonwealth's Attorney's Office on here."

"That's correct," she says, straightening her spine. "And believe me, I've thought hard about adding it."

"What on earth would make you think Neil Tory should be on this list?"

"For starters, he's my ex-husband and we didn't part in the best of ways. I have reason to believe—and he's given me every indication—he intends to make my life difficult."

"What makes you say that?" he asks, now appropriately interested.

"Until our divorce I had a very successful career with a large firm in Norfolk, while Neil worked for his father in the Commonwealth's Attorney's Office in Richmond. Then in a span of months, I went from one of the firm's top trial lawyers to sitting second chair, and finally I was treated like no more than a legal clerk. My ex-husband and his father are golfing buddies with my firm's partners."

She'd mentioned last night their divorce had not exactly been amicable but I didn't realize the extent of it until now.

"Are you implying—"

Reagan holds up her hand to cut the detective off.

"That's not all. Almost seven months ago I left the firm and struck out on my own here in Suffolk, figuring it was the only way to get a fresh start. Next thing I know, Neil transfers to the Suffolk Commonwealth's Attorney's Office and takes a seat at the prosecutor's table in my first major trial here.

"He won that first one, but a few weeks ago we faced off in the courtroom again, and this time the jury acquitted my client. Needless to say that didn't go over well."

"Do you have reason to suspect he would resort to something like arson?"

"Before yesterday I would've said no, but then I discovered he's the prosecuting attorney on the bullshit case against Cal."

Finally Melville's eyes, which had been glued to Reagan, come to me.

"Yes, I understand Mr. McGregor is in some hot water."

I try not to react and leave the talking to Reagan; she's much better at it than I am. I trust her blindly. Still, I hope she's cautious with what she shares with Melville because for all we know he's close with Walker.

"That will all be sorted by tomorrow's pretrial hearing. In fact," she adds with a cool smile, "it might be informative for you to drop by."

"Is that so? If there's time I may just do that." He glances back down at the list when suddenly his eyebrows shoot up. "I see you have a Sean Davies listed. Who is he?"

The question is asked casually but I sense the tension behind his words. Apparently Reagan does too as she seems to weigh her words carefully.

"Mr. Davies is a client. In fact, I represented Mr. Davies in the trial I just mentioned. He was acquitted."

Melville rests his elbows on the table and folds his hands, leaning slightly forward.

"I'm afraid I don't understand; if you managed to get Mr. Davies off, why add him to the list? It doesn't make sense. He should be thrilled with you."

The challenge seems to make Reagan uneasy, and I lightly press my knee against hers in a subtle expression of support.

"It was actually my assistant who insisted his name be added. Mr. Davies expressed interest...in me," she adds almost shyly. "In an attempt to spare his feelings, I'd politely informed him it would be unethical for me to go on a date with a client. I should've been clearer, because he showed up with flowers and the wrong idea the day after the verdict. It was an uncomfortable situation."

"He hasn't been in touch since? You haven't seen or heard from him?"

"No."

Suddenly Melville turns to me. "How about you? Do you know Mr. Davies?"

A restless feeling comes over me and I struggle not to squirm under the man's scrutiny.

"I don't. I've never seen the man, although I did see the flowers in Reagan's office, as well as his signature on the note."

"Note?"

"*Hope we see each other again soon. Yours, Sean,*" Reagan quotes.

The detective leans back, tilting his chair and placing both hands on his head.

"Well, this is an interesting development," he mumbles, his eyes on the ceiling.

Reagan glances over at me with a questioning look. I shrug; I have no clue what's going on.

"Detective?" she finally prods. "I'm afraid I'm at a bit of a loss here?"

"Right," he says, straightening in his seat. "Remember I mentioned I had a new case pop up in the early hours of the morning? A man on his way to his early shift backed out of his garage, into the alleyway, behind his house and almost ran over the body of a man. We don't have confirmation yet—unfortunately his face was beyond recognition—but according to the driver's license in the man's wallet, he was a neighbor."

Under the table I grab Reagan's hand.

"The name on the license was Sean Davies."

"Oh my God..." She covers her mouth with her free hand.

"I'm waiting for a warrant so I can search the house. We'll need something to confirm the body's identity. Do you know of any family members? Spouse? Children?"

Reagan shakes her head. "From what I know he was married but divorced many years ago. He told me he had no children. That's all I know."

She turns to look at me.

"I feel so guilty now for even considering he might've—"

"Ms. Cole," Melville interrupts, drawing her attention. "I wouldn't feel too guilty if I were you. We found a switchblade in his pocket and the smell of gasoline still lingering to his clothes."

CHAPTER THIRTEEN

Reagan

"Relax, Slick. You've got this."

Cal's hand covers my wringing ones.

The truth is, I am nervous, or maybe I should say unnerved. Yesterday's visit to the police station threw me off. In my line of work, I'm not a stranger to violent crime, but the idea Sean Davies—a man I'd seen and talked to not that long ago—was brutally beaten and killed is chilling. According to Melville, the coroner suspected he had been killed between twenty-four and thirty-two hours prior to his body being discovered. All that time his body was lying in the alley.

I was also shaken to find out it looks like Sean was the one to set fire to my office and vandalize my car. I can't wrap my head around that. One day you think you have all the answers, only to discover you never really knew anything at all. Doubt followed closely after.

Last night I tried to put all that out of my head and focus on the pretrial hearing today, but even curled up in bed with Cal holding me, I was questioning myself.

"I know. It's just, there's so much going on, it's rattled me. I'll be fine though," I quickly add, realizing I probably shouldn't be worrying my client. He's also someone I've come to care about more than I should, which is why I need to be on the ball. I know for a fact, Neil will not be pulling any punches.

When we drive up to the courthouse parking lot, I carefully remove Cal's hand from my lap. "I should've called a cab," I point out. "It's probably not smart to arrive in one vehicle."

"You're overthinking. The likelihood of anyone thinking twice about a lawyer and her client arriving in the same vehicle is slim to none," he responds calmly.

He's right; I'm being paranoid.

I calm myself while he looks for a parking spot, but when we walk into the building and I catch Neil watching me through slitted eyes by the door of the courtroom, my nerves are back.

During a pretrial the onus is on the prosecution to present evidence to convince the judge there is sufficient merit to their case. It's also an opportunity to present pretrial motions, like the ones I have in front of me.

I'm not surprised when Neil focuses in on the security tape, making a big production of showing it on the large screen TV rolled into the courtroom. I know Judge Raymond and am familiar with the fact he does not take kindly to dramatics in his courtroom, but Neil may not be aware. He's big on theatrics, hence the oversized screen and emotional narration of Krista Hardee's statement of the events simultaneous to the video playing.

"Mr. Tory," Judge Raymond interrupts him. "This isn't an audition for the school play. Can we dispense with the melodrama? I can see the screen quite well and have a copy of Ms. Hardee's statement in front of me. I assure you I'm able to put the two together."

Neil darts a quick glance in my direction, and I have a hard time not smirking. Apparently Cal doesn't feel the need for any such restraint since he loudly snorts his amusement, which earns him a sharp look from the judge.

Neil takes his seat, but the moment the tape comes to an end he jumps to his feet.

"As you can see quite clearly, Your Honor, not only did the defendant drag the victim across eight states, he ruthlessly assaulted her in full view of security cameras." He grabs a folder from his desk and hands it to the bailiff. "These pictures taken of the defendant days after the incident illustrate the desperation with which the victim tried to fight off her violent attacker."

Judge Raymond proceeds to flip through the file.

"Three pictures? These are all you have in evidence?" he asks, his eyebrow raised.

"Yes, Your Honor."

"Mr. Tory, far be it from me to tell you your job, but if you wish to convince me a violent attack took place at the hands of the defendant, I would expect to see more than what—given the lack of additional evidence—appears to be violence done to him."

"But, Your Honor, the video clearly—"

Judge Raymond holds up his hand to shut Neil up.

"Other than the video, is there any tangible evidence you can present that illustrates a violent attack on Ms. Hardee? Any images of bruises she may have sustained, a rape kit that might have been taken. Anything at all?"

"Your Honor, Ms. Hardee was distraught—"

"Simple yes or no answer will do, Mr. Tory; is there any evidence, other than this video, to support Ms. Hardee's complaint."

"No, Your Honor."

"Very well. Ms. Cole?"

To say the judge looks less than impressed with the case would be an understatement. I'm ready to put the nail in the coffin my ex manufactured himself.

"Yes, Your Honor. I have a motion to suppress the video evidence the prosecution presented."

"On what grounds, Ms. Cole?"

I hand the bailiff a copy of the motion and a copy of the USB-key with my recording.

"On the grounds that the evidence is incomplete. As you can see from the images attached to the motion, the camera feed the prosecution had you review is only one of several cameras focused on that particular area of the parking lot. Copies of those additional camera feeds might have made it clear that Ms. Hardee was not fighting off Mr. McGregor, but rather the other way around. Also attached are copies of my multiple requests to Detective Walker, as well as the prosecutor's office, for release of those additional video feeds, without success. On the USB-key you will find confirmation by a security guard at the jail there are a total of three cameras focused on the area where Mr. McGregor's vehicle was parked that night."

From the corner of my eye I can see Neil jump to his feet, but Judge Raymond is faster.

"Not a word, Mr. Tory." Then he turns to me. "Is that all?"

"No, Your Honor, I also have a motion to dismiss."

"Let's see it." I hand the folder and my second USB-key over to the bailiff who delivers it to the judge. "Another one of these?" He holds up the key.

"Yes, Your Honor. That is a recording of Oliver Hardee admitting his daughter is romantically involved with Detective Walker."

"Objection, Your Honor!" Neil is on his feet, wildly gesturing. "Defense is looking to...to..."

"Mr. Tory, just a reminder this is merely a preliminary hearing, not a trial. I'll need some time to review and we'll reconvene tomorrow morning at nine thirty. Court's recessed."

The moment Judge Raymond's gavel comes down and he disappears into his chambers, Neil grabs his files, tucks them under his arm, and storms out of the courtroom.

I sink down in my chair and throw Cal a big smile.

———

CAL

"Fuck, but you're magnificent."

She looks a little shell-shocked when I release her mouth, but when I move in to kiss her again, she holds me off with a hand against my chest.

"Sally's here," she says, turning to look at her house where we just pulled up.

"Pity." I grin at her and take the keys from the engine. "Celebrations will have to wait 'til later then."

"I make it a rule not to celebrate before the verdict is in. It brings bad karma."

She throws a saucy grin over her shoulder as she jumps out of the truck. I follow suit and catch up with her at the steps up to the porch, wrapping an arm around her waist as I lean in close.

"We won't call it a celebration then," I mumble against the shell of her ear, "but it will involve both of us naked."

"Mmm, we'll see," she teases, pressing her ass into my groin.

I'm about to feel her up on her porch when the door swings open wide.

"You're back already?" Sally stands in the doorway, grinning big. "Is that good news?"

Reluctantly I let go of Reagan and she walks inside as she gets her assistant up to speed. I stay on the porch, pulling out my phone while I adjust myself. Pooja picks up on the second ring.

"How did it go?"

"We'll know tomorrow morning. Court's been recessed until then." I turn my back to the house and take in the view from the porch. "Anything from Dean?"

"Yup. He found the skip, but ran into some resistance from local law enforcement."

"Where is he?"

"Up in them there mountains; some small dot on the map on the South Carolina border with Georgia."

"Does he need help?"

I won't be able to go myself until my own situation is resolved, but Mark could go down if he needs a hand. Dean may be only half Jamaican—the other half is German—but all people see is a large black man, and believe it or not, in some areas that can make our job a bit more challenging.

"No, he says he has it under control, but it'll likely be Wednesday before he gets back."

"Good. Anything else pressing?"

"Nothing we can't handle. So you're not coming back here?"

"Think I'll work from here."

"Sounds good. Oh, Boss? Mark wants a word."

I hear rustling in the background and then Mark's voice comes on.

"Did you get my message?"

I glance at my screen and notice a message waiting.

"Sorry, had the phone on silent in court and forgot to switch it back on. What's up?"

"Hoped I would catch you before court this morning, but remember that gym Walker has a membership for? I thought I'd poke around the place early this morning and hit pay dirt."

"Walker?" I guess.

"Yes, but you'll never guess who was spotting him on the bench press. Looking pretty chummy too. I watched them for about twenty minutes. The conversation looked intense."

I roll my eyes, even though he can't see it. "Killing me here," I grumble.

"Right. None other than your lady's ex. Neil Tory."

His contact in the prosecutor's office.

"No shit."

"None. I was too far to hear. I hung around after both were gone and tried to get a little more information from the girl at the shake bar. She said she's seen them work the weights together before. Sorry I couldn't get more."

"Not to worry. This is fine."

All the pieces are starting to fit into place.

Walker must've gone to his buddy, Tory, to push through the charges against me. Whether he was pissed I apprehended his girlfriend, or perhaps was trying to make Krista look more like a victim for leverage in her upcoming trial, it doesn't really matter. What matters is he found a willing ear in Tory as soon as the man found out his ex-wife—the one he'd just lost a big case against—was listed as my lawyer.

The one thing I can't figure out is how the torching of our building and the subsequent murder of Reagan's client comes into play, but something tells me it's all connected.

———

"Okay," Reagan says thoughtfully, as she picks up our empty plates and dumps them into the sink.

I just shared my thoughts with her over dinner. She'd been busy with Sally in her office this afternoon and I was able to get caught up on some work myself. Then I ran out, got a few groceries, and ended up cooking dinner while she was finishing up her day.

Anything to get to the celebration part of our day faster. It's well overdue.

"But what would've connected those two in the first place?" she continues, her back to me as she runs water in the sink. "You say Walker transferred from Norfolk sometime last year? Neil came to the Suffolk office sometime in the fall. He was in Richmond before. I don't see the connection. I know Walker didn't work on the Davies case or I would've met him before."

I step up behind her, reach around, and turn off the water with one hand, while the other splays wide over her stomach, pulling her body against me.

"No more work," I whisper with my lips against her ear. "We've come to the fun part of our day, I've waited long enough."

I slide my hand from her stomach down and under the waist-band of the lounge pants she changed into before dinner.

"Fuck, Slick," I hiss when I find out she hasn't bothered to put on panties.

Nothing but soft skin, a tidy patch of trimmed hair, and warm wet folds. The moment my fingers brush her clit, she groans and drops her head back on my shoulder.

"So warm, so fucking wet for me."

She inhales sharply when I broach her entrance, sliding first one, and then two digits inside her tight channel. Her hips rock against me as I press the heel of my hand against her clit. With my other hand I manage to unbutton my jeans, shoving them partway down my ass. Then I pull down her pants and she grabs onto the sides of the sink, tilting her ass.

When I sink inside her, I glance up at our reflection in the kitchen window; her mouth open, the blush I love dark on her cheeks, and her eyes burning with heat for me.

Magnificent.

CHAPTER FOURTEEN

Reagan

"I'm not going to take up much of your time."

We wait for Judge Raymond to sit before we do the same; only Neil stays standing.

"Your Honor," he says, a smug look at me before he turns to the bench. "I have reason to believe—"

"Mr. Tory, take a seat please. Like I said; I won't waste your time, the way the prosecution has wasted this court's."

I try hard not to smile. Those words are music to my ears. Even though I didn't think any judge worth his salt would've continued with this farce, you never know until he makes his ruling. From the corner of my eye I see Neil sitting down, his head turned to the back of the courtroom. Waiting for someone?

"I've given you the benefit of the doubt by merit of the office you hold, Mr. Tory. However, after going over the original complaint, the police report, the video you provided, as well as the recordings and motions from the defense, I'm afraid I had more questions than answers. As a result, I took it upon myself to do due diligence, something I would've expected from you." Neil is pinned with a glare and I see him squirm in his seat, still nervously darting glances over his shoulder. "I had copies of all the jail's security feeds for the date in question dropped off at my office yesterday afternoon."

That gets Judge Raymond Neil's undivided attention, and mine as well.

"The only thing I haven't decided yet is whether I should let this go as just shoddy work on your part and grant the defence motions, Mr. Tory, or whether to add charge of prosecutorial misconduct for you."

Behind me the doors slam open and turning around, I see Detective Walker marching into the courtroom.

"Your Honor, before you make any rulings on misconduct," Neil says, jumping to his feet and reaching over the railing to grab an envelope Walker hands him. "I have evidence of misconduct on the part of the defense attorney, Ms. Cole, who is involved in a relationship of a sexual nature with the defendant, Mr. McGregor."

Judge Raymond drops back in his chair and lifts his eyes to the ceiling.

"You have got to be kidding me."

I'm stunned. Too stunned to even speak although I should probably have objected at some point, but this is playing out like my worst nightmare.

I watch helplessly as Neil hands the bailiff the envelope. There isn't currently a rule that prohibits a client/attorney relationship, however, it's not exactly ethical and therefore is frowned upon. Any goodwill I might have had with Judge Raymond may have just blown up in my face.

"*Fuck*," I hear Cal hiss beside me, but my eyes are focused on that damn envelope, wondering what the hell he might have in there.

This time when the judge leans forward, his sharp glare is for me. The bailiff slides the envelope in front of the judge, who slaps a hand on top. After what feels like fifteen minutes of his scrutiny, but was probably just a few seconds, he shoves the envelope back.

"Take this to Ms. Cole and have her take a look at it first."

"But, Your Honor," Neil almost whines.

"Mr. Tory, I've had it up to here with you. Sit down and be quiet or I'll hold you in contempt." Then he looks into the spectator gallery. "Detective Walker, I believe? Take a seat.

"Ms. Cole, I'm afraid to ask..."

"Yes, Your Honor. I *am* in a relationship with a good friend of my brother's, my landlord, my neighbor, and yes, Callum McGregor is also my client."

It's not exactly a lie, but the timing is questionable, something I'm pretty sure Judge Raymond can smell a mile away, given his narrowed eyes on me.

I lower mine to the envelope and slide the handful of pictures from the envelope, gasping when I get a look at the first one.

"Sonofabitch," Cal growls, pushing up from his seat.

I grab for his arm and yank him back down.

In the photograph, I'm clearly outlined in my own damn kitchen window and Cal is visible behind me. Thankfully with my shirt in place, but from the look of bliss on my face there is no way to misinterpret what we're doing.

"Ms. Cole," Judge Raymond calls me to attention. "Where were those pictures taken?"

"At my home, Your Honor. Last night, through my kitchen window at the back of my house. We had a reasonable expectation of privacy, given that my backyard butts up to the wildlife refuge."

I don't bother adding that my house is set back from the road at such a distance; you wouldn't have been able to see much had we been naked on my front porch. It's not illegal to take pictures of someone in a public setting, or if in full view of a public space like a sidewalk, but that was clearly not the case here.

"I see." He nods, rubbing a hand over his face before he looks up at the prosecution table. "Mr. Tory, I'm at a loss as to what your motivation may have been to resort to these levels to discredit, or distract, or whatever the hell you think you were doing..." His voice rises with every word as he tears into Neil, who fruitlessly attempts to get a word in during the judge's tirade.

I'm unsteady on my feet when we finally walk out of the courtroom, clutching the envelope with damning pictures, and Cal's hand at my elbow. I should be thrilled, getting all charges against Cal dropped, but instead I feel like I just climbed out of a particularly dirty sewer.

"I need a shower," I tell Cal when we step out on the sidewalk.

"All I need is few minutes alone with those pieces of shit," he growls in response as we approach his truck.

"Please don't." I turn to face him, and slide a hand along his jaw. "Getting you out of trouble once was enough. I have no desire to head back in court for seconds."

————

CAL

I'm still seething when we get to Reagan's place.

Don't get me wrong; I'm relieved the judge dismissed the charges against me. What I'm seeing red about are those fucking pictures, taking a private and intimate moment I shared with a woman I've fallen fast for and dirtying it.

I can handle people throwing shit at me—in my line of work it happens more often than not—but the lengths to which Reagan's ex and that dirty cop went to discredit Reagan pisses me right off. Having the judge threaten both those bastards with an investigation into their professional conduct doesn't quite satisfy me. I want to know why.

"Are you gonna be okay here?" I ask Reagan when we walk in the door. "I've got a few things I want tackle back at my place."

"Sure," she answers easily, placing a hand in the middle of my chest. I cover it with mine. "I'll be fine. Sally's here and if I don't have a ton waiting for me, I might even go out and garden for a couple of hours."

I lean my forehead to hers. "I'm sorry," I whisper, knowing she'll understand what I'm apologizing for.

"Don't," she whispers back. "Maybe I'll make a potato salad, we'll throw a few steaks on the grill, and make a bonfire after. Burn those damn pictures and take back that amazing memory."

I can't help the grin. "Amazing, huh?"

"Oh please, you don't need that large ego of yours stroked," she teases. "You know it was."

Instead of answering I kiss her hard.

"I might want seconds."

"Don't push your luck, handsome, it won't be in front of that kitchen window." She gives me a little shove and I reluctantly let her go, but not before I get the last word in.

"Maybe not, but I recall a nice big mirror over your bathroom sink."

———

"Need your help on something, Muff."

I don't even bother trying to keep my conversation with Jackson private. There's not a lot my guys don't know about me.

"What's up?"

I fill him in on what's happened since the last time we spoke, ending with this morning's events in court. Not my first choice for him to find out his sister and I had sex in the kitchen, but those pictures make it impossible to avoid.

"You have got to be fucking kidding me."

"Wish I were and as much as I hate those goddamn pictures, I'm more worried about the why. If a prosecutor and a police detective—neither with any real marks against their records—do something like this, how far are they willing to go?

What is their motivation?" I share what Mark told me about what he saw at the gym. "Clearly there's something tying these two."

"I'll find out," Jackson says with confidence. "I'll put my guys at Cole Security on it. Leave it with me."

I want to object but the truth is, when it comes to tracking my guys may be top of the line, but for digging up dirt Cole Security is better equipped.

"Fair enough," I concede.

"You look after Reagan."

"No need to ask," I bite off, annoyed.

"Yes, I fucking do—she's my sister."

With that he ends the call, and when I look up I notice every eye in the room on me.

"What?"

Moe is the first to speak up. "In front of the kitchen window, dude?" A stapler sails across the room at his head. "Hey! Watch it."

"You're an idiot," Pooja scolds him, getting up to retrieve her stapler. "First the woman has her tires slashed, her office lit on fire, and then someone's in her backyard snapping pictures? Maybe you should focus on that."

My office manager is probably the most even-tempered, kind woman I know, but Moe has the ability to draw blood from a rock, spouting his inappropriate comments. He's a good guy, but sometimes has trouble with his filters. In that he doesn't seem to have any.

Mark stays silent, observing Pooja as she seems to decimate the much larger, louder man with just a few words.

"Where is she?" he finally asks me.

"Reagan? At her place, with her assistant."

"You heading back there?"

"Planning to as soon as I'm done here. Why?"

Mark shrugs. "Nothing I can put my finger on. There's just something off about this whole thing."

I'm still thinking about Mark's words when I'm on my way back to Reagan's place an hour later.

I sent her a text to let her know I was on my way when Pooja eventually made me leave. She promised she'd keep the guys in check and would have Dean call me the moment he got in, so there was no reason for me to hang around.

The first thing I notice when I drive up to her house is the single car parked out front. Only the Kia, Sally's car is gone. Immediately all the hair on my neck stands on end.

I slam the truck in park and hop out, jogging up the front steps. The door is unlocked.

"Reagan!"

I check the office but it's empty. She's not in the living room or kitchen either. Upstairs?

I take two steps at a time and check the bedroom, then the bathroom and even the spare rooms, but she's not there.

"Reagan!" I call out again, my heart pounding out of my chest as I run back down.

Did someone come in? Did they take her? I didn't notice any signs of a struggle, and I'm pretty sure Reagan would put up a fight. Where the fuck is she?

I'm trying not to panic and force myself to take a good look around. Her keys are on the hall table, her purse on the floor underneath, and when I walk to the kitchen I see her phone on the island next to a bag of potatoes and a cutting board.

Then I spot the sliding door open a crack and my eyes are drawn outside, to the edge of the swamp. It wouldn't take much to disappear out there. I step out on the deck, my gaze focused on the tree line when I catch movement from the corner of my eye.

"Hey. You're home already?" Reagan steps out of the side door of the garage, carrying a hose and a sprinkler, and walks over to the faucet on the outside wall. I sink down on the steps with relief while I listen to her talk. "I had to dig around for these. The hose had fallen off the hook and was stuck behind some of the boxes. I wanted to put the sprinkler on while I'm cooking."

She finally notices I haven't answered, drops the hose, and walks up to me.

"Are you okay?"

I lift my head and look into those gorgeous hazel eyes.

"Where's Sally?"

She seems genuinely surprised.

"She got a call from the school. Matt's not feeling well so she left early to pick him up. Why?"

"Because you were out here alone. Your fucking front door was unlocked, the back door open, and for all I knew you could've been dragged out into the swamp."

Understanding washes over her face and she looks remorseful.

"I knew you were on your way because you texted me. I left the door unlocked so you could come in. I'm fine."

She reaches out and ruffles my hair like I'm twelve years old. I should be pissed, but all I can feel is relief as I grab her by the hips and pull her on my lap.

"You're getting a goddamn dog."

CHAPTER FIFTEEN

Reagan

"I'm not getting a dog," I say for the third time.

Matt flops back on my couch, his headache and fever almost forgotten.

Sally has kept him home from school since Tuesday, but her babysitter wasn't available today. When she called this morning, I told her she could bring him here, and he could hang on my couch while we worked. I love Matt. He and Sally are like family.

I feel a little bad for Cal, though. He was out for a bit this morning, but since he got back it didn't sound like he got a lot of work done. Matt's been talking for most of the past hour. I came out here to grab a coffee and maybe distract the boy for a bit, when he cornered me about a dog.

"Come on, Auntie Reagan, you live out here by yourself. Think of all the fun a dog could have here."

"I don't have time for a dog, Matt."

I throw a dirty look at Cal, who's chuckling at the dining table and suddenly I don't feel bad for him anymore. Bastard, he's guilty for starting this. He's been on my case for days now.

"Besides," the boy continues, "Mom used to say you were too busy for a boyfriend too, but you got one of those."

"Matt!" Sally yells from the other room and Cal bursts out laughing, causing the boy to giggle.

I try to keep a straight face but when a beet-red Sally comes barreling in, looking at her son with murder in her eyes, I lose the fight.

"Great," she grumbles, throwing her arms in the air. "Blood, sweat, and tears to teach this one some manners, and you two encourage him."

She promptly turns on her heel and stomps back to the office.

"Sorry," I call after her, only making Matt giggle harder. "You..." I point my finger at him. "You're trouble, mister. Watch your show."

Cal winks at the boy before turning a grin to me. "Majority rules, Slick."

"My house, my rules, Mac," I lob back, as I make my way to the coffee pot. "And if you want a dog so badly, get one yourself."

"Yeah!" Matt, who closely watches the interaction, cries out.

Wonder how long it'll be before the kid starts bugging his mom for a dog of his own. I shake my head while I pour myself a refill and make my way back to my office, ignoring the male bonding going on in my living room.

"Too busy for a boyfriend, huh?" I tease Sally when I sit down across from her.

"The kid can't remember to put his socks in the laundry, even though I remind him on a daily basis, but he recalls something I mentioned in passing months ago," she says, dropping her head in her hands. "During a discussion on why everybody doesn't have a boyfriend like Corbin Becker's mom does." She lifts her head. "For some context; Amy Becker landed herself a hunk of a firefighter, who drags her kid everywhere. He was hounding me to get a boyfriend so I may have brought up the fact you didn't have one either. Just so you know, I don't make a habit of discussing your love life—or until recently, your lack thereof—with my ten-year-old son."

"No worries," I assure her with a smile, but that last remark earns her a little revenge. "You know, you could always get *him* a dog."

The horror on her face is immediate and I stifle a chuckle.

"Ohhh, you wouldn't."

"I might," I shrug, "It would help get the heat off me."

That earns me a dirty look, but Sally doesn't get a chance to say anything when my phone rings.

"Reagan Cole."

"Ms. Cole, it's Detective Melville. Do you have a minute?"

"Sure. What can I do for you, Detective?"

"Two things actually. I wanted to let you know we've closed the arson investigation. We found evidence confirming Sean Davies was the one to vandalize your car and set fire to your office."

"What kind of evidence?" I'm curious to know.

"Some forensic evidence, but we also found a stack of journals in Mr. Davies' house. His last entry is about a fantasy scenario describing pretty much what happened at your office, but he ends up a knight in shining armor saving the damsel."

I shake off an unpleasant shiver running down my back. Scary to think what that kind of delusion might've led to.

"Okay, but then who killed him?"

"That's the thing," Melville muses. "I've been working from the premise these are two separate cases, but I'm starting to think they're connected."

"How?"

"That's the million-dollar question I was hoping you might help me with. Now I may be reading too much into this, but I've been asked by my chief to take over a colleague's caseload, who was suspended from duty a few days ago, and going through his notes your name pops up."

My ears perk up when I realize who he's talking about.

"You mean Walker?"

"Yes, I'm afraid he doesn't like you very much."

I snort. "That doesn't surprise me. Along with the prosecutor —who happens to be my ex-husband—he tried to railroad Cal McGregor on a bogus charge and discredit me at the same time, but that seems to have backfired on them. If Walker is anything like my ex, he'd be looking for outside sources to blame. Me being the preferred target."

"But there is nothing indicating Walker knew Sean Davies or had any connection to him," Melville states before he falls silent, like he's waiting for me to fill in the blanks.

I rack my brain. The only connection would be through Neil, who was on both cases and is apparently friendly with Walker, but that still doesn't give either a reason for harming Sean. Or does it?

Neil has always been the passive-aggressive type, prone to bursts of temper but never physical. He never struck me as a violent person, unless you count the sharp edge of his tongue. I can envision him doing a lot of bad things, but killing someone? And why?

"My ex was the prosecutor in both the Davies case and also this recent farce. I've recently learned from an acquaintance he's on friendly terms with Detective Walker—they apparently frequent the same gym—but I can't really see how that would be important to your case. I leave that to you to figure out."

From a legal perspective, it's probably better for the detective to discover these things in his own investigation, even if I did point a finger in the right direction.

"It's been a while since I worked out," Melville says. "Maybe it's time I get back into it."

I smile and look up at Sally, who's been following along closely.

"May not be a bad idea, Detective."

———

CAL

Cute kid.

I lift a hand in response when he waves from the back seat of his mother's car. He hadn't been happy when Sally declined an invitation to stay for dinner, but she put her foot down, telling him it was time they get out of our hair.

I'm secretly glad, because sharing space with Reagan without being able to touch her the way I'd like to was proving difficult. I thought I had more restraint than that, but she is proving me wrong. Or maybe it's just her.

Part of me wonders if it's the chaos we seem to have landed in which makes melding our lives together so easily. It really shouldn't be, considering we haven't known each other that long, and are both used to our own space. Still, this past week has been almost effortless.

We work during the days and have quiet nights at home, enjoying the sunsets out back, a lot of talking, making out, and inevitably we roll into bed together. Nothing special and yet more meaningful than anything I can remember.

I've always been restless—a little wild even—it's one of the reasons why the adventure of the military drew me in. When that didn't end the way I'd hoped, bounty hunting was a good replacement. With this job I never know what the next day brings, or where I'll end up. The fact it's unpredictable is a big part of the attraction, and yet here I am, hoping my phone won't ring tonight.

A hand slides along the small of my back and Reagan ducks under my arm, snuggling into my side.

"Everything okay?"

I give her shoulders a squeeze. "Yeah." I turn her away from the open door and close it before walking into the living room.

"I feel like pizza." She tilts her face up to me and I drop a kiss on her mouth.

"I'm good with that. Want me to order?"

While I call, Reagan goes upstairs to put on something more comfortable. I hope that means something with an elastic waistband. By the time she comes back down, pizza is on the way, and I'm waiting outside with a couple of beers.

I lean my head back and she bends down, kissing me sweetly before she takes the seat next to mine.

"So..." I grab her hand and play with her fingers. "Rescue or breeder?" I grin when she pulls her hand back and her eyes throw daggers at me.

"I'm not getting a dog," she snaps.

"I know, you told *me* to get one."

I snag her hand again and, despite the stubborn look on her face, she lets me entwine our fingers. A moment later I have to let her go again when my phone rings in my pocket. When I fish it out I see it's Jackson calling.

"Your brother," I announce before answering. "Hey."

"Detective Marshall Melville. Recognize the name?" Jackson asks right off the bat.

"Hello to you too, I'm sitting here with your sister so I'm putting you on speaker, and the answer is yes."

"Reagan's there?"

"Hey, Jackson, what's up?" she says.

"Detective Melville, I just got off the phone with him."

"You did? I talked to him today as well. Why were you talking to him?"

"Cal called me Tuesday, told me what happened in court, and I've been looking into Tory and Walker."

I'm at the receiving end of another emasculating glare from Reagan. I didn't mention I'd spoken with her brother, and I'm guessing that's a firm no. I make a mental note not to keep things from her in the future.

"Find anything?" I ask Jackson.

"Oh yeah. One of my guys has a contact in the Commonwealth's Attorney's Office in Richmond. Rumor around the watercooler has it Daddy Tory caught Neil doing drugs in the office and they had a big fight. Not long after, he was moved to the Suffolk office."

"Neil? Drugs?"

It's clear Reagan had no idea, judging by her reaction.

"Yup. Remember Jenna Dolinsky?"

I have no idea who he's talking about, but apparently his sister does.

"His college buddy. She was at our wedding. I don't even know if they stayed in touch, though."

"They did. They were living together while he was in Richmond."

I hear Reagan's gasp and when I look over her face has paled. I guess that was news to her.

"How long..." she starts asking, but then shakes her head. "You know what, I don't wanna know."

"No, you don't," Jackson says in a sympathetic voice.

That stupid motherfucker cheated on Reagan? That piece of crap is not worth the dirt on her shoes.

"Is there a point?" I ask abruptly.

"Yeah, she confirms he had a drug problem. Apparently they didn't part on good terms because the woman was spilling all the dirt. Including the name of his dealer. A woman he'd met at the country club by the name of Krista Hardee."

Neither of us interrupts as Jackson goes on to explain how he contacted the chief of police at the Suffolk PD and was passed on to Detective Melville. He ended up talking to him at length, outlining his findings.

Even after he ends the call, we sit quietly side by side, each lost in our own thoughts while we sip our beers.

"I can't believe I didn't know," Reagan finally says, sounding stunned. "I used to think of myself as relatively intelligent, but now I feel like such a fool."

"Hey..." I turn to her and cup her face, those beautiful eyes looking dull. "Addicts are the best liars. You know this."

"Still. What does that say about me?"

"No, you don't take this on. This says nothing about you and everything about him. I knew he was a loser for letting a treasure like you go. He's the fool in this scenario."

She blinks a few times and I see the life come back to her eyes.

"You need to stop being so damn amazing," she says in a scolding tone. "You're already irresistible enough."

"I am?"

A blush darkens on her cheeks as she smiles almost shyly.

"Don't tell me you don't know you already have me falling hard."

I pick up her hand and kiss her palm.

"Then my job here is done," I tell her just as the doorbell rings announcing the arrival of dinner.

Grinning, I kiss the top of her head before getting up to get our pizza.

"Don't look so smug," she fires off over her shoulder.

CHAPTER SIXTEEN

Reagan

Having my hands in the dirt feels wonderful. It's been my favorite way to de-stress and think since I bought this place.

I've been doing a lot of thinking since Jackson's phone call Friday night. I stopped loving Neil a long time ago, so why does it feel like betrayal? It's not like I thought there was much redeemable about the man before, but what Jackson uncovered still shocks me. It taints the few good memories I was holding on to, but also makes me question my judgment. I've always been able to tell myself when I fell in love with him he was a different man. Now I wonder if that was ever true. What if it turns out he was responsible for Sean Davies' death? A few days ago I wouldn't have been able to imagine Neil getting his hands dirty like that, but I'm not so sure anymore.

I grab my wheelbarrow and head to the next bed. My garden is a combination of flowerbeds and raised vegetable planters. I've already been able to eat some of my own beets, kale, and onions. Beans will be next; I'm guessing another week or so.

It's peaceful out here, no traffic noise, no neighbors mowing the lawn, just the sound of birds from the swamp.

I'm about to start weeding around the tomato plants when I hear the sliding door open.

"We've got company, Slick," Cal calls out.

I left him on the couch watching baseball when I went outside earlier. Such a domestic scene: cooking a late breakfast when we finally got out of bed, cleaning the kitchen together, and then Sunday afternoon sports. Much the same pattern followed in many households, I'm sure. I know it was in our house growing up.

"Who is it?"

I'm trying to think of who might show up at my door on a Sunday afternoon, when Detective Melville steps out behind Cal. I quickly hustle to the hose to wash the dirt of my hands and wipe them dry on my jeans before I join them on the deck.

"Sorry to barge in on you on a Sunday afternoon, but I have a few questions."

"Not a problem," I tell the detective. "Can I get you a coffee?"

"Already offered, Sweetheart," Cal mumbles, tucking me under his arm the second I'm within reach.

"Thanks, but I'm trying not to take up too much of your time."

"Well, at least have a seat," I offer.

He sits down and I take the other chair, Cal perching on my armrest.

"I received a call from your brother on Friday."

"Yes, he told me."

"Good, that saves me explaining why I'm looking into your ex-husband. I'm currently investigating his role in the handling of Mr. McGregor's case. We spoke with Ms. Hardee, and we already have Walker on a seventy-two-hour hold but we haven't been able to locate Tory. Any thoughts on where we might be able to find him?"

It's on my lips to tell him I don't have a clue, but then I remember his father's hunting cabin. He spent many a men's weekend there while we were married, but I hadn't seen the place once.

"His father has a cabin not far from Roanoke, but I'm afraid I couldn't tell you where exactly. I've never been there."

"I can find out," Cal offers, but Melville waves him off.

"Appreciate the gesture, but I'm sure you understand the need to do everything by the book. I told Ms. Cole's brother the same thing when we spoke. Luckily, we have Judge Raymond on board, who is more than a little upset a mockery was made of his courtroom. I'm sure we'll have the necessary information in no time."

"Fair enough."

"There's one last thing before I let you get back to your Sunday. It's been bugging me. I know your ex lost the case against Davies, but I can't really see a reason he would want to kill the man. Walker has talked some, but stays adamant he knows nothing about Davies. I'm having a hard time coming up with a motive."

"I'm sorry, I can't help you there," I apologize to the detective. "Maybe Sean knew something? Saw something? I'm grasping at straws, I really have no idea."

Melville nods and gets to his feet.

"Only person with answers is Mr. Tory. All the more reason to chase him down. I'll leave you folks to it and if there's any update, I'll let you know."

"Much appreciated," Cal answers for both of us. "I'll show you out."

I head back to my vegetables and start yanking at weeds, lost in thought. I suddenly want for all this to be over. I was always passionate about my work but with everything that happened this past month, I'm losing the stomach for it. Maybe it's time to find another way to put my law degree to good use, although I'm not sure what direction to take. Perhaps all I need is an extended vacation. I don't remember the last time I've taken one. Even our honeymoon was no more than a long weekend in Myrtle Beach.

I catch a rustle in the grass and am about to turn around

when a blow snaps my head sideways, and takes my knees out from under me. I gasp at the blinding pain but before I can open my mouth to scream, the lights go out.

———

CAL

"My offer stands," I tell Melville when I walk him to his cruiser. "Anything that'll help you get and keep that lowlife behind bars."

He lowers his head to hide a grin.

"So noted, but let me reiterate the need to keep this investigation clean. Tory has some major connections with ample legal muscle, including but not limited to his own father. Any case against him has to be airtight and beyond reproach, or they'll make mincemeat out of it."

"Fair enough. It's just that tracking is what I do best," I explain. I don't mention that I want this shitshow over with so I can enjoy my relationship with Reagan without pressure from every side.

"Trust me, I get it, and I'll promise to keep you up-to-date." He opens the driver's side door. "I best get going; I have a person of interest to locate."

I give a rap of my knuckles on the roof of the cruiser as he climbs behind the wheel, and I turn back to the house. Inside the game is still on TV and a quick glance at the clock shows it's time for a beer.

I grab a couple and glance out the window to see if Reagan is still on the deck. I can't see her, but the side door to the garage is open. She keeps her garden tools in there so she's probably grabbing something. I stick one bottle back in the fridge to keep it cool and twist the top off the other, taking a swig while my eyes drift to the game playing on the TV in the living room.

I'm not even sure what inning they're on, and I'm not sure I really care at this point. I turn away and pull open the freezer to see what we can throw together for dinner. It's steak or chicken. I walk to the sliding door and stick my head out.

"Reagan? You want steak or chicken for dinner?"

I listen for a response but hear nothing.

"Reagan?"

Setting my bottle on the railing, I make my way down the steps and over to the garage. I poke my head in and call her name again, but she's not in there. Cold tendrils crawl up my spine as I turn back to the yard. Her wheelbarrow is still parked by the vegetables.

"Reagan!"

I take the steps up to the kitchen and storm inside, heading straight upstairs. This is like fucking déjà vu. I remind myself last time I panicked she was fine as well. I'm sure she's fine now too. She'd better fucking be.

She's not upstairs either and I stop to look out her bedroom window to the yard below. That's when I spot it, a piece of fabric or something, at the far end of the yard where the trees start.

I have my phone in my hand and am already dialing as I barrel down the stairs.

"Reagan's gone," I manage out of breath, as I tear out of the house and to my truck.

"Where are you?" Mark asks right away, and in as few words as possible I tell him how I was just saying goodbye to the detective and when I came back she was gone.

"Seconds," I whisper, as I grab my gun and a folding knife from the glove compartment. I shove the knife in a pocket and automatically check to make sure the gun is loaded, even though I feel like I'm losing my mind. "I swear I was out here only a few seconds."

"Cal, get a grip, my friend. Are you sure you've looked—"

"I don't have time for this," I cut him off, shove the phone in my back pocket, and start running around the side of the house to the back.

I know what it is before I even touch it. A makeshift sap or slungshot; a sock filled with sand or gravel lying on the edge of the grass. A quick and easy weapon used to knock someone out.

The panic that was seizing me is washed out by the wave of rage. I see red at the thought of someone touching Reagan, let alone hurting her. I'm sure she was dragged into the swamp but I have to keep my head about me, I can't just charge in blindly.

Forcing myself to slow down, I let my eyes scan the edge of the trees and the underbrush, looking for anything out of place. A scuffed piece of bark, a broken branch, a crushed leaf—any evidence of someone trampling through.

There—a flash of red. I make my way closer and see one of the flip-flops Reagan was wearing earlier. My instinct is to rush right in but I don't know how far my phone signal will last out here, so I quickly retrieve my phone and hit redial.

"On my way," Mark says without introduction. "I got hold of Melville and he turned around. He should be there any minute."

"Don't have time to wait around. You'll find a red flip-flop about twenty yards to the right of a massive oak, halfway down the tree line behind her yard. I'm going in."

"Fuck," I hear him swear. Not something you'll hear often from him. "Mark your trail."

I feel for the knife in my pocket.

"Will do."

CHAPTER SEVENTEEN

Reagan

My head pounds.

I blink my eyes open but everything seems to be moving, causing my stomach to revolt so I quickly close them. It takes a moment to orient myself. I'm being moved, my body bouncing in rhythm to the crunch of footfalls.

Someone is carrying me. Every footstep is one farther away from safety.

A large hand clamps down on my leg the moment I start struggling.

"*Fuck.*" The deep grumble is one I don't recognize and my body freezes.

I open my eyes again, fighting down the accompanying nausea as I try to focus on the body carrying me. All I see is a pair of jeans-clad legs and mud-covered boots.

"Close enough," he mutters to himself, and the next moment I feel myself sailing through the air.

I land hard on my back, the air forced from my lungs on a cry. I squint to get my first glimpse of the looming figure standing over me, but his face is in shadows. I blink a few times to clear my vision.

"Who are you?" I croak. "What do you want?"

He barks out a phlegmy laugh.

"Figures you wouldn't remember me, you arrogant bitch. So blinded by your own righteousness, you're as big a piece of shit your clients are. Protecting the scum of the earth from getting what they rightly deserve. You're no better than them. You may be smarter, dress in them fancy clothes, and think you're high and mighty, but you ain't fooling me."

"I don't know—"

My words stick in my throat when he leans down, his menacing face coming into focus. I remember him now and fear paralyzes me when he speaks.

"Dragging upstanding citizens through the slime, ripping apart good people, letting criminals walk. Well he didn't go far, did he? Was watching that motherfucking coward torch your place." Spittle hits my face and I try to scramble back, but I don't get far. "Beautiful. Only thing better woulda been had you been inside. Take care of ya both at once."

I have the trunk of a tree at my back and his hot breath blowing in my face.

"You killed Sean."

"Shoulda taken my time. Enjoyed it more," he sneers. "*You* I'm going to tear apart strip by strip." My heart stops when he pulls a large knife from his belt and brings the tip to my face. "Like you did my Sheila's reputation." He seems fascinated by the trail his knife leaves behind on my cheek and down my neck. I'm afraid to breathe too deeply. "Wasn't sure where to find ya until that lawyer pointed me here."

"Lawyer?" I whisper.

"That useless, sniveling cocksucker was supposed to nail that murderer's hide to the wall. So full of himself, telling me not to worry. He deserved what he got too." Another phlegmy bark of laughter. "The weasel led me right here. Tried to bargain his way out of what was coming and gave you up like a bad habit. Drove his own car up a back trail and walked me straight to your yard. Then I took care 'a him."

My head is spinning trying to process what he's saying, and when the penny drops I can't help the gasp. The man is deranged.

"What did you do to him?"

Suddenly he fists a handful of my hair and pulls me up, the knifepoint pricking my throat. He never lets go as he starts walking, but on my feet I at least have a chance to get away. As long as I can get that knife away from my throat.

A splash when something slides into water nearby has him momentarily distracted and no longer feeling the sharp point of the blade on my skin, I react. Flying on adrenaline, I turn into his body, aim my fist for his nuts, and at the same time yank my hair from his hold. Ignoring the sharp sting on my scalp, and the man's loud bellow, I swing around and start moving my feet as fast as I can.

Somewhere along the way I've lost my flip-flops, and I feel the wet ground slick between my toes as I run my eyes in front of me. Then I hear him holler, he's closer behind me than I thought, and I make a fatal mistake—I turn my head.

I catch sight of him at the same time my foot catches on something and I stumble, desperately trying to stay upright, but there's no stopping the momentum. I hit the ground and immediately try to scramble back up, when my hand encounters something soft and pliable. I swing my head around and find myself staring into a familiar pair of dull eyes. I scream, let go right away and—my pursuer momentarily forgotten—I crawl backward, away from my ex-husband's lifeless body.

Then I hear his voice behind me, just as my hand closes around a branch.

"I see you found him."

———

CAL

I try to keep my footfalls as silent as possible as I make my way through the dense trees. My gun is tucked in my waistband at the small of my back and I hold my knife in my hand, carving a quick X in the closest trunk every twenty or so paces. My ears alert to each little sound as I try to ignore the drumbeat of my heart.

Fear is not something I've felt often in my life, despite some of the hairy situations I've encountered, but right now it's keeping my chest in a firm vise. My instincts want me to barge through the swamp, and only by the thinnest thread am I able to let experience guide me.

I force down mental images of Reagan hurt or even dead, and desperately hold on to reason. The fact whoever grabbed her didn't kill her right in her garden, but took the effort to drag her into the swamp, gives me a glimmer of hope. If it was that ex of hers, I vow to tear the weasel apart, limb by limb.

Forty-five years old and I'd long since made peace with the fact I'd be alone. No wife, no children, no family of my own, and although it had given me pause at times, I've been content with my life and my freedom. In the relatively short time since I've met Reagan, content doesn't seem nearly enough.

I love her.

It seems fast, but even before I knew her, I'd known of her. Through childhood stories Muff would share, the sister he'd so proudly speak of. Over the years there'd been plenty of opportunities to bump into her but somehow that never happened. I wasn't even at my friend's wedding, I'd been hot on the trail of a skip back then.

I can't help think there was a reason it took this long for us to meet. A sense maybe the moment was never right before. It is now, but I'm terrified those few seconds I took my eye off the ball may have cut our time too short.

I lift my knife and cut another X in the bark when I hear a

howl deeper in the dense woods. My ears pinpoint the sound off to my right, and I immediately turn that way. No longer concerned with being heard, I charge through the brush, ducking under branches, in the direction the yell came from.

One wrong step and I trip, my artificial knee giving out on me as I crash to the ground. I disregard the pain, pulling myself up on a tree trunk, but my leg will barely hold my weight.

A piercing scream freezes the blood in my veins before adrenaline kicks in. That was Reagan and she's not far. My knee forgotten I stumble toward the sound.

I see him first. His back is turned and he seems to be struggling with something. Or rather someone, as I see when he swings around, holding Reagan in front of him. At first I'm relieved to see her alive, but then I notice the large hunting knife at her throat.

Immediately my hand goes to the small of my back for my gun, but it's not there. *Fuck.* I must've lost it when I went down.

It's not Neil; that much is clear. Blood streams down his face from a gash at his temple but his eyes are sharp and focused on me.

"Any closer and I'll cut her."

Reagan, who'd been struggling in his hold, suddenly stills and her eyes find me. I lock in with mine, conveying as much as I can without speaking.

They're about twenty feet away, and I don't have a gun. All I have is the knife still clutched in my hand. No way I can do much with that unless I get closer. I stealthily slip it in my pocket.

"You won't get out of here," I call out, taking a cautious step forward. "In a few minutes these woods will be teeming with law enforcement."

"Bullshit!" he yells. "I ain't falling for that."

I take another step. "That's too bad, because you've got only one way out and that's to let her go."

"Not gonna happen!"

"Look..." I raise my hands, palms out, as I take another surreptitious step. "Whatever your beef, it's not worth going to jail for," I try. "You can still walk away from this."

The laugh he barks out chills me to the bone. It's the sound of someone who's already committed himself.

"Yeah? And what about him?"

He nudges his head to the ground beside him and that's when I notice the prone body of a man by his feet, half hidden in the brush.

"Hey," I call out, desperate to keep him talking as I inch my way closer. "What's your name? I'm Cal."

"What the fuck does it matter?"

I hold my breath, as he seems to adjust his grip on Reagan, whose eyes never waver from me. The knife is pushed harder against the soft skin of her throat and I see the fear, but also determination, on her face. If there is any way I could get him to let up on his hold, even for a second, I know she'll fight to get away.

"It matters. It matters a lot. Why don't you tell me why you're here?"

I pick up the sound of a branch snapping to my right, and so does he, his eyes immediately scanning. I grab the opportunity.

"Over here!" I yell loudly, hoping to disorient him.

His head snaps back to me, but the hand holding the knife seems forgotten, the blade no longer cutting into Reagan's neck. All it takes is a slight nod and she drops down.

I'm already moving when I hear the sharp report of a gun and the man goes down, his torso pinning Reagan to the ground.

From the corner of my eye, I see Detective Melville stepping out from behind a tree, but my focus is on my woman. I grab the man's shoulder and roll him off her.

"Slick, Sweetheart?"

She's covered in blood and I can't tell if it's hers or his, but her eyes are open and panicked.

"She okay?" Melville asks from behind me.

"Reagan, talk to me." I rip my shirt over my head and start wiping at her face.

"Holy fuck," she finally says, her voice hoarse.

Ignoring the two dead bodies on the ground beside her, I haul her up in my arms and bury my face in her dirty hair.

"For a few seconds there I thought my heart stopped," I mumble, feeling her hands on my chest.

"It's still beating."

CHAPTER EIGHTEEN

Cal

Dammit.

I glare at Mark's back, and I just know the asshole is laughing his ass off.

He and Dean showed up as I was looking Reagan over for injuries, while she relayed what happened to her and who the dead man next to Neil Tory was. I didn't recognize the name, but Melville did. Apparently he'd been on the list Sally and Reagan had put together for him, but somewhere near the bottom. My focus had been on Tory and Walker; I hadn't even paid attention to the rest of the list.

The knife had sliced Reagan's chin when she let her weight drop her to the ground, and I found a good-sized lump to the side of her head. Aside from that, she had some cuts on her feet from running through the swamp on bare feet. I wasn't going to let her walk and I tried to lift her but my knee didn't hold out under our combined weight.

I had no choice but to let Mark carry her out, while Dean stayed behind with Melville until his reinforcements show.

"I can walk now," I hear Reagan say when we walk out of the tree line and onto her grass.

"You put her down and we're gonna have issues," I call out to Mark, whose responding chuckle only worsens my mood.

I follow him up on the porch where he carefully lowers Reagan in a chair. I shove him aside and pull a second chair in front of her, sitting down as I pull her feet on my lap.

"Where can Mark find your first aid kit, Slick?"

"Laundry room off the kitchen, up on the shelf." Mark has barely disappeared inside when she turns to me. "You know, I actually think I should have a shower first."

I take in the state of her face and her hair.

"I know you didn't want us to call the EMTs, but you may need stitches, Sweetheart."

"All the more important I have a shower now," she insists, a stubborn set to her bleeding chin.

Before I can stop her, she swings her feet to the floor and pushes out of the chair.

"Wait. Your feet."

"My floors are clean, Cal, and I'd rather walk."

She takes a step and I see her wince. I stand up and grab her arm, pulling it around my neck as I slip my own around her waist. I'm rewarded with the hint of a smile as I support her inside the house.

"Where are you off to?" Mark asks, just coming out of the laundry room with a basket he drops on the island.

"She's having a shower," I answer for her.

Mark blocks our path. "Here, let me carry you."

"Fuck off, Phillips. I've got it."

Reagan snickers. "Now, now, boys. Thanks, Mark, but I think I'll walk."

Like a ten-year-old I feel like sticking out my tongue, but instead I raise an eyebrow at Mark, who steps out of the way.

"Why don't you put some coffee on?" I throw over my shoulder as we pass him.

We make it upstairs and into the bathroom.

"I've got it from here," she says, keeping her face averted.

"You sure? I was going to hop in with you, wash some of this swamp dirt off me."

"I'm sure."

For all her earlier bravado and lighthearted joking, she sounds flat now. Drained all of a sudden. I gently manipulate her chin so I can look her in the eye. Her usual sparkle has dulled and the strain is suddenly visible on her face. I'm guessing the adrenaline is wearing off and it's all going to hit her at once.

"Okay," I whisper, dropping a soft kiss on her lips before I pull the door closed.

I grab some clean clothes for myself, and head to the second bathroom down the hall. I'll be fast and I'm not planning to go far. I'll give her some time, but I'm gonna make sure I'm close by if she needs me.

After a quick rinse off, I step into the hallway and walk over to her bathroom door, putting my ear against the door. At first all I hear is the water running, but then I hear something else and without hesitation, I push the door open.

REAGAN

I could feel it coming, the meltdown.

I quickly wash my hair, and allowing the shower to beat down on me, I let go of the tight control and the tears flow. When my body starts shaking so hard I'm afraid my legs won't hold me up, I sink down in the tub, holding my knees.

I'm not sure how long I sit there when the door opens and Cal slips in, sinking down beside the bathtub with his back against the wall. He doesn't say anything, doesn't interfere, he just sits there—looking straight ahead—and yet his presence calms me.

When I lift my head and reach over my shoulder to turn off the faucet, he gets up. He slides the shower door open, reaches for my hand, and helps me step out. Then he pulls a towel off the hook, wraps it around me, and finally he folds me in his arms. My wet hair is getting his clean shirt wet.

"Your shirt."

"It'll dry," he rumbles, slowly stroking my back until he finally asks, "Did that help?"

"I don't cry a lot." I feel his hand still on my back and I lift my head so I can see his face. He looks puzzled. "I mean, I know it's a turn-off for most guys. I didn't want you to think I make a habit of it."

Now he looks pissed.

"I'm not sure where you get your information but for the record, I don't give a flying fuck if you cry. Cry all you damn want but don't block me out."

That shuts me up.

I'm so used to hiding emotions, I automatically withdrew when I knew I wouldn't be able to hold them back. Most men I know would run at the first sight of tears—hell, Neil did until I stopped crying in front of him—but not Cal. He was hurt I shut him out.

I wrap my arms tighter around him and burrow my face in his chest, no longer caring I'm getting him wet. He doesn't.

Suddenly I'm bone-tired. I feel him press a kiss to my head before he takes a step back.

"Why don't you go lie down for a bit?" he suggests gently, and I'm struck by how tuned-in he is. I never said a word but he instinctively seems to know what I need.

"What if they need to ask me more questions?"

"They'll be busy out there for a while yet. I'm going to run downstairs to get the first aid kit, why don't you get into something comfortable in the meantime?"

When he walks into my bedroom minutes later, I'd just laid down on top of my covers. Silently he checks the cuts on my feet and puts on some antibiotic ointment before covering my feet with the socks I left on the bed. Then he tilts my head back and checks out the cut on my chin, which seems to have stopped bleeding.

"It's not that deep," he concludes. "You can probably get away with a couple of butterfly bandages."

"There's wound glue in the basket."

He digs it out and carefully applies it before pressing the edges together. Then he covers it with a large Band-Aid.

"Get some sleep," he whispers, his face hovering over mine. "I'll leave the door open a crack, so you can call if you need me."

"Thank you for being so good to me."

His lips brush mine.

"Thank you for letting me."

Then he packs everything back in the basket and leaves the room.

I close my eyes but instead of falling asleep, I see the events of this afternoon play out in my mind. The smells, the sound of Winters' voice, Neil's dead eyes staring at me. The stark fear when Winters caught up with me, and panicked I swung that branch my hand found at his head. It wasn't enough to stop him, but it did injure him and it got him very, very angry.

My hand comes up to cover my neck remembering that cold blade. I expected any moment I would feel it slicing through my throat.

Like a movie it plays through my mind again, and again, until finally—exhausted—I fall asleep.

CAL

"She okay?"

Mark is in Reagan's office, where he's taken over Sally's desk, when I come back downstairs.

"Still sleeping. Have you heard from Dean?"

It's been a couple of hours and they'll be losing daylight soon.

It'll be darker still under the canopy of the trees. Dean, who stuck close to Melville, has been texting us a few updates. We know they found the trail where Tory's car was parked. Rather than track through Reagan's property, they've been using that same trail to bring in the crime tech unit and more recently the coroner's van.

"He says they'll be another half hour or so. Coroner just left with the bodies."

Good, that'll give Reagan a little more time to sleep because I'm pretty sure Melville will stop here after. My eyes catch on a picture frame on the bookshelf behind her desk. A snapshot of Reagan and Jackson at some outdoor event, both of them laughing.

I spoke with Jackson after leaving his sister to rest. I didn't want him to find out what happened through the grapevine. Turns out, he was on the East Coast for some meetings both in New York and at his office in Norfolk. He'd planned to check in with his sister before heading back home, but I'm pretty sure he'll be here sooner than later, wanting to make sure she's all right. Reagan may have a houseful by the time she wakes up.

"We should get some food. A couple of pizzas or something easy."

"I can go pick some up," Mark suggests, shoving his chair back before getting up. "Probably faster than waiting for delivery out here."

I head to the laundry room after he leaves, switching the load from the washer to the dryer. I'm washing both our dirty clothes. They were caked in mud and covered in blood, and I didn't want to leave them lying around as a stark reminder of what Reagan went through this afternoon. I'm sure it'll be seared in her mind as it is.

I'm just washing a few dishes in the kitchen when I hear the front door open. An unusually disheveled Jackson walks in. He normally looks like he just walked off the pages of *GQ*, but not today. His dark hair looks like he's been running his hand through it and his face looks gaunt.

"Where is she?" is the first thing out of his mouth when he sees me. A little too loud.

"Watch the volume, she's sleeping."

He immediately makes a move to the stairs, but I manage to grab his arm.

My friend makes for an imposing figure, he's only a couple of inches taller, but even that rumpled suit jacket can't hide the buff body underneath. I'm no slouch myself, but I don't spend nearly as much time keeping my physique in top shape. I like my beer and my takeout too much. Muff could probably take me down in a heartbeat.

From the look he shoots me, it's clear he's about two seconds away from reminding me of that fact.

"I said she's sleeping. She doesn't even know I called you yet —something I'm sure I'll catch flack for—and the last thing she needs is another shock today."

"She's my goddamn sister," he growls, his eyes shooting fire, but I'm not standing down.

"And she's my woman, which is why I'll go up in a minute and give her a heads-up we've got company."

"We?" he sneers.

My own temper is flaring, but because I get where he's coming from I'm staying calm.

"Yeah, we. My stuff is in her closet, my toothbrush in the bathroom, and right now our clothes are sharing the dryer, so yes—we."

As quickly as it flared, the anger disappears, leaving him looking tired and worn.

"Is she okay?"

I told him over the phone already, but I get he wants to look me in the eye when I repeat she's fine.

"Come have some coffee."

Without waiting for an answer, I turn and head to the

kitchen. A large hand drops on my shoulder as I'm getting another mug from the cupboard.

"Sorry."

"It's all good. Have a seat and I'll fill you in on the latest."

Leaving Jackson looking a little less ragged and a lot more calm, I head upstairs.

She's curled on her side, still sleeping, but the moment I sit down on the edge of the bed her eyes shoot open.

"Hey."

The little smile accompanying the sleepy voice is encouraging and I lean over to kiss her forehead.

"Sleep okay?"

"Yeah." She rolls on her back and looks at the window. "Oh my God, it's nighttime. How long did I sleep for?"

"Couple of hours. I came to wake you up because it looks like Melville may be heading this way soon. They're almost done out there."

I hate the reminder deepens the soft lines on her face instantly.

"Okay, I'll get up."

She flicks back the covers right away, and I make room so she can swing her legs over the side.

"Also," I continue, "I called Jackson earlier." I know she's annoyed when she turns a glare on me and I hold up a hand. "You know your brother, he has eyes everywhere and I didn't want him to find out from anyone else."

Understanding dawns on her face and she nods. "Good call."

"Yeah, what I didn't know, though, is that he's on this side of the country. In fact, right now, he's sitting in your kitchen."

"He's here?" Her face lights up and her eyes go to the door.

"Having coffee."

She gets to her feet and moves toward the door, but I pull her back and wrap my arms around her.

"What?"

"Kiss," I mumble, dropping my mouth to hers. Her hands fist

in my shirt as I feel her melt against me. "Also," I add, when I lift my head, "before you rush down, you may wanna freshen up first."

She instantly pulls out of my hold.

"Are you saying my breath stinks?"

I have a hard time not cracking a smile, but I have a feeling it might cause damage to some of my favorite parts if I do.

"You'll probably feel better," I try for diplomacy.

I guess I have a bit to learn in that department when she spins on her heel and—as much as her bandaged feet will allow —stomps off to the bathroom.

By the time I follow her, she already has her mouth foaming as she glares at me in the mirror. I bend my head so my mouth is at her ear.

"I love you," I whisper, before dropping a kiss on the tender part of her shoulder.

I back out of the room, leaving her with her toothpaste-covered mouth open. Just as I turn to head down the stairs, I hear her call after me.

"Callum McGregor! Don't tell me that when I'm pissed!"

CHAPTER NINETEEN

Reagan

"Morning."

Two heads turn in my direction when I walk into the kitchen. Cal is by the stove, cooking something that smells amazing, and Jackson is sitting at the island, a mug of steaming coffee in his hand. I head to my brother first and kiss his cheek.

"You sleep okay?" he asks in his familiar rumble, looking a lot better this morning than he did last night.

"Like a baby."

I'm not lying. Despite my nap yesterday afternoon, I'd been exhausted again by the time Detective Melville and Cal's guys left. Jackson had crashed in the spare bed after shooting a sharp look at Cal's back as he walked ahead into my room.

When I'd come downstairs yesterday, I'd barely had a chance to greet my brother before the detective and Dean came in through the sliding door. Mark showed up not long after with a stack of pizza boxes he dumped on the dining room table.

Cal had slapped hands and barked at the guys when they fell on the boxes like a pack of hungry wolves, making sure I had food in front of me first. I noticed Jackson was observing this closely.

While eating, Melville—who'd asked to be called Marshall by

this time—gave us a rundown of what they found. The men didn't appear affected when he explained the extent of damage done to Neil, but I quickly lost my appetite.

The coroner would do a proper autopsy this morning, but in his preliminary findings he'd mentioned my ex-husband appeared to have been tortured for some time before Winters finished him off. A fate—had Cal not found me—would undoubtedly have befallen me.

More enlightening had been the discovery of Neil's car, which proved to be a treasure trove of evidence to be used against Walker in court. Dead men can't talk, but my ex's briefcase did all the talking for him.

They'd found a phone they'd been able to access using his own thumbprint—a detail that sent shivers down my back—revealing text messages between Walker and him. Threats of exposure and disbarment if Neil did not cooperate. He may not have been a particularly good lawyer, but he was meticulous. Aside from the telling text messages, he also had a legal pad with handwritten notes in his chicken scribble inside his briefcase, giving a more complete picture.

From what Melville could piece together, Walker had been the one to first make contact with Neil, on behalf of Krista Hardee. He'd already been in hot water with his father at the Richmond office, and the last thing he needed was to be exposed in a drug trial.

The knowledge my ex-husband had been forced into collaborating with a crooked cop and his drug-peddling girlfriend, nor his subsequent death, did much to alleviate my disgust for the man. He made his bed. Unfortunately for him, while he was looking in one direction to avoid justice, it caught up with him from another at the hands of Winters.

I walk over to Cal, slipping under his free arm as I press myself to his side.

"Whatcha cooking?"

"Your favorite." He smiles down at me.

"Stuffed French toast?"

"What else?"

I rise up on my toes and meet his lips for a sweet kiss.

"You keep taking care of me like that, I'll be double my size in no time."

He shrugs. "More for me to love."

He told me last night when I was pissed, and I didn't have a chance to come back to it, but there are no such distractions this morning.

"Good. And for the record, I love you too."

He drops the spatula on the counter and wraps both arms around me, a smile in his eyes.

"Figured you might," he says, as he takes my mouth and kisses me thoroughly. I wrap my arms around his neck and hold on for dear life as he...

"Ahem."

I feel Cal's lips pull in a smile against mine before he lifts his head, turning to look at my brother who made the sound.

"Problem, Muffin?"

"That's my baby sister you're mauling," he protests, a scowl on his face.

"And?" I contribute, challenging him. "I was mauling him right back."

"Don't need to fucking see that on an empty stomach," he grumbles. "Ruins my appetite. Although the declarations of love were bad enough. You've known each other how long?"

Now he's pissed me off and I'm working up a good head of steam.

"A: I'm forty years old and long since stopped being a baby anything. B: How many times have I walked in on you and your wife going at it? Even after you already had the girls. And finally, C: just because you took forever to get your head outta your ass before settling down with Catherine doesn't mean everybody else should diddle around."

I feel Cal shaking with suppressed laughter but I keep my

angry eyes on my brother. I notice with some satisfaction he at least looks a tad sheepish.

"Diddle?" Cal repeats, now laughing out loud, which earns him an elbow in the ribs.

Then the front door opens and Sally walks in, stopping in her tracks when she spots my brother.

"Jackson? What the hell did I miss?"

———

CAL

"He's right, you know?"

I can feel her eyes on me as I leisurely stroke my fingers up and down her arm.

We're out on the back deck, watching the sun go down. I'd been afraid at first she might have negative associations out here, but other than a long look at the wheelbarrow still standing next to her vegetables, it doesn't appear to bother her.

Jackson left earlier, he had business to take care of in Norfolk before heading back home, and I'd been highly amused by Reagan's teasing. She gave him grief about how he'd better not wait another six months before showing his face, and if he dared show up without his family again, she wouldn't let him in.

I'm an only child, so I don't know the play between siblings, but these two—as much as they can bicker—love each other a ton.

They hugged on the front porch, her brother getting her back with threats of calling their mother, so the minute he took off, she ran inside to grab the phone. That resulted in a long conversation I was reluctantly drawn into for a FaceTime introduction to the parents. Both firsts for me: FaceTime, *and* meeting the parents. Probably a good thing she threw me under the bus, because if I'd known in advance I might've made myself scarce.

Her mom is sweet, but I can sense the spine of steel underneath, much like her daughter. Dad is former Air Force and
grilled me relentlessly on my background until his wife finally
put a stop to it. She promised as soon as her husband was feeling
better, they'd come for a visit.

That's when I suggested out loud we could go visit them
instead. Another thing that is apparently not done without
discussion, as I found out later. Her mother jumped on it and
had us commit to a weekend in July. I realized after we got off
the phone and I got an earful from Reagan, that apparently 'it's
hotter than hell' in Arizona in July.

I finally pacified her with a cold beer and the promise of a
beautiful sunset out here.

"Who's right?" I ask.

"My brother. It's been how long?"

"Does it matter? Time is irrelevant when it feels right.
Besides, neither of us is getting younger."

Her hand hits me square in the solar plexus.

"Speak for yourself," she grumbles. "I still can't believe I fell
in love with you in a few short weeks."

I pluck her hand off my chest and press a kiss in her palm.

"Sweetheart, it only took me seconds to fall ass over teakettle
for you."

That earns me a sweet smile before her eyes drift off into the
distance again.

"Still," she persists stubbornly.

I only hesitate for a second before I decide to lay all my cards
on the table.

"Sweetheart, I'm forty-five years old. I've been on my own
since my uncle passed away. I'd come to terms with the fact the
traditional trimmings of life wouldn't be part of mine. No one
had ever interested me enough, no one ever stirred those needs,
and within days of meeting you face-to-face for the first time, it
was all I could think about.

"So no, it's not too soon. It's been a long time coming and

I'm ready. I don't want to waste time. I don't want to leave your bed to go back to my own, I want to be able to make you French toast every damn morning if that's what *you* want. I want to dig in the dirt with you, talk about work, and I wanna get a dog. I've never had one." She's smiling now, giving me the confidence to take it one step further. Full disclosure. "I also never thought about kids..." I hold up a hand when her eyes pop wide open. "But I'm thinking about them now and I don't know how you feel about that. It isn't a deal-breaker because I have more with you than I've had before, but it's something I think about."

Even as I'm rambling on Reagan started saying something but I missed it.

"Sorry, what was that?"

"I'd given up on kids," she repeats in a soft voice. "I wanted them but I also wanted my career. I thought I could have them both, but Neil didn't agree. He thought I should stay at home and raise kids. I always thought it would be a partnership."

I shift in my seat and take her face in my hands.

"Right here, right now, let's agree we don't talk about him anymore. He doesn't get to play any part in what we have, or do, or discuss." She nods. "Who says you can't have both? When I say I want kids, I don't just mean I want to father them—although I like that part too—I want to be a father to them. We'd share responsibilities, work out a schedule. Heck, I've thought about letting the guys do the bulk of the tracking and chasing. I'd rather come home to you every night."

She shakes her head. "Callum McGregor, what are you doing to me?"

I grin at her.

"Laying it all out. Stuff other people take years to figure out, we're clearing up in seconds. So what's it gonna be, Slick? Wanna take a few chances with me and jump in the deep end? Get a dog?" I lean a little closer. "Make a couple of rugrats?"

"This is crazy," she mutters, smiling nervously as the familiar flush creeps up on her cheeks.

"Probably, but the only rules we need to live by are those we set ourselves. Everyone else can fuck off."

I can see the answer in the big smile on her face and the sparkle in her eyes, but I still want to hear her say it.

"Okay…"

"Okay, what, Sweetheart? I need the words," I push her.

"Okay, I'll jump into the deep end with you."

The words are barely out of her mouth when I have her on her feet and start pulling her into the house.

"Hey! Where are we going?"

I grin over my shoulder at her.

"To celebrate in front of that big mirror in your bathroom," I tell her.

The sound of her soft giggle behind me as I lead her through the house settles deep in my chest.

———

"Hurry, Slick."

I look at the reflection of her slack mouth and feverish eyes as I pound into her from behind.

The tingle starts at the base of my spine and I know I won't be able to hold out for long. I slide a hand between her legs and find that small bundle of nerves, rolling it under the pads of my fingers.

"Come for me, baby."

Sweat drips in my eyes and I blink furiously to clear them, not wanting to miss a single thing.

"Cal, my God…please…"

I buck my hips wildly and press down hard on her clit, her body clamping around me like a vise. I plant myself deep inside her, the roar of my voice joining her cries.

Nothing like it. Bare, skin-to-skin, slick with sweat and sex, and those beautiful eyes locked on mine, echoing love. The dream of a child hanging in the air between us.

CHAPTER TWENTY

Reagan

"It's bigger."

Sally looks at me with her eyebrows raised.

"I know, Cal decided to bump out the back since the wall and roof had to be rebuilt anyway."

We're standing in what is our freshly painted and reconfigured office. With the extra space in the back, we were able to add in a filing room behind the kitchen and the conference room is actually a proper-sized space now. The front is much the same, except my office now has glass walls and a door. Without the filing cabinets in that space, there was enough room. With my door open I can still see and hear Sally, but I can have privacy if I want by closing the blinds.

"Guess it pays to date the landlord," Sally teases.

I can't argue that. Cal also made sure an updated security system was installed, although I did draw the line at cameras inside my offices. He had some kinky ideas around that, but I told him it'd be a hot day in hell I'd take off my clothes in my office, let alone in front of a camera.

"Did you say Matt's with his dad this weekend?"

Sally rolls her eyes.

"Yeah, making up for last weekend when he bailed last

minute. I think he has a new girlfriend. Matt mentioned something."

I observe her closely. "You don't seem too broken up about it."

"Hell no. I just wish he'd stick with one instead of introducing a different flavor every month. Matt's going to think that's the norm. Already he's collecting girls like baseball cards."

I wince. "Well, he's a cute kid."

"Trust me, I know. Some days I secretly wish he develops a temporary case of acne from about twelve to eighteen."

I follow her down the hall to the kitchen. Not much has changed there, except for a fresh coat of paint. The carpeting throughout has been replaced with a rubber laminate and other than a few light fixtures left to install, the place is move-in ready.

"What do you think about opening the office back up on Monday?" I ask her.

"Does that mean moving over the weekend?"

"Unless you have plans. I mean, Cal's guys are moving back in over the weekend as well. I'm sure they'd be willing to give me a hand."

She shoots me a half-grin. "Twist my arm, why don't ya."

"You're incorrigible," I chide her, but it falls on deaf ears. Her grin widens and she nudges me with her shoulder.

"Nothing wrong with looking. They're a smorgasbord of man-candy."

From behind us I hear a throat clearing. Both our heads swivel around to find Mark leaning against the doorway, a suggestive smirk on his face.

"Can't say I've ever been referred to as a buffet before," he says, laying the British accent on thick.

"Never said I was talking about you," Sally huffs, as she pushes past him.

I bark out a laugh before slapping my hand over my mouth.

"Ouch. I do believe I've just been told," Mark mutters, grabbing his chest as he watches Sally walk away.

"She's all bark and no bite," I share, patting his arm as I move past him into the hall. "Don't take it personally."

———

"We need to talk about this move," Cal says that night, sitting out on the deck watching the stars.

Many nights in the past month have been spent out here, relaxing after dinner and learning more about each other with each day.

"What about the move?"

He turns to me and grabs my hands, slipping his fingers between mine. Cal turns out to be very tactile. At least he is with me, and the biggest surprise is I actually like it when he grabs my hand when we're out and about, or just sitting here in the back-yard. I get the sense it's more about needing the connection than anything else.

"Moving back into the office means my apartment becomes available again."

My stomach cramps and a sour taste surges up in my throat. I'd wondered once or twice but when he never brought it up, I made myself believe things would stay as they are. I love having him here—and I thought he felt the same. Could I have been that wrong?

"What's wrong?" I can feel him looking at me but I can't bring myself to turn my head. "Slick?"

I clear my throat and force myself to say in a clear voice, "I guess it makes sense. It's a great apartment. Close to everything. You could even walk to work if you wanted to."

"Sorry?" He sounds pissed and I turn to glance at him. He looks pissed too. "You're telling me you want me to head back to my apartment?"

"No," I quickly answer, a bit confused as I shake my head to clear it. "I mean, I thought that's what—"

"What I was gonna suggest is, since we'll have enough hands

on deck, we get the rest of my stuff over here," he interrupts. "We can store it in the garage, sort out later what to do with it, but I want the apartment empty so I can put it on the market."

"Oh."

"Yeah."

He still looks annoyed when I get up and climb on his lap, his arms automatically wrap around me.

"You're moving in," I say with a smile.

"Sweetheart, I thought I already had."

———

I'm surprised when Sally shows up with Matt in tow Saturday morning. The poor kid looks as miserable as his mother looks ticked off.

"What happened?" I ask her when he's out back, playing with Buddy, our new rescue pup.

Well, maybe pup is not the right description to use on the six-month-old calf galloping through the backyard. He's of undetermined lineage and has a few habits we need to train out of him, but he makes up for it with his loving disposition. We picked him up at the shelter earlier in the week, the day after we discussed our living situation.

"Matt's father..." she uses air quotes, "...decided last minute it wasn't a good weekend after all. Didn't even have time to tell the kid himself, just said to tell him he'd see him next weekend." She dumps a stack of files in the box with some force. "God, he's such an asswipe."

We're in my office packing up. It made more sense for the guys to tackle Cal's apartment first. They'll move the stuff to his office, pick up his personal belongings and furniture, and bring it here. That'll give us time to get things here packed up for them to take back to town.

"Poor Matt," I commiserate.

"He'll be okay. He's been begging me to bring him over to

meet Buddy every day since I told him you got a dog."

The sound of the sliding door and then dog feet scratching my wood floors gives us seconds to brace for the rambunctious topic of conversation. Buddy does everything with a certain level of enthusiasm.

"Easy, Buddy,"

I caution him when he comes tearing around the corner, sending the small area rug in the hallway sailing into my living room. Matt is not far behind.

"Mom, can we—"

"Matthew," Sally says in her parental voice, hands on hips. "Did you wipe your feet?"

He immediately looks down at his shoes that look far from clean.

"Sorta, but Mom—"

I press my lips together to hold back the snicker.

"And close the door behind you?"

The boy groans and rolls his eyes before jogging back to the kitchen. We can hear the sliding door slam shut.

"Mom," he's already talking as he walks back. "Can we have a dog?"

I earn a dirty look for the snort that escapes me. To keep the peace I come to her rescue.

"How about you first practice on Buddy? See if you've got what it takes to look after a dog?"

"Sure!" His grin is wide and face hopeful.

"Awesome. So first you'd need to learn to clean up after him. We scoop his poop once a day. There's a shovel against the side of the house and a bucket." I have a hard time not laughing at the way his expression just drops.

"Okay, Auntie Reagan," he says grudgingly, his shoulders drooping as he walks off.

I feel a little guilty for busting his bubble, but then Sally more than makes up for it.

"You would so rock as a parent."

CAL

I'm about to head over to pick up Reagan when I hear her door slam. I watch some kid wearing his goddamn pants hanging off his ass awkwardly walk to a souped up Honda Civic, with a mail-order spoiler kit on the trunk.

"Who the hell was that?" I ask her, when I open her door and find her in front of the window, watching the Honda peel out of his parking spot.

"That was Emmet Licker." She turns to me with a grin. "My client."

"Yikes."

"I know," she says, putting her hands on my chest and lifting on her toes to press her lips to mine. "Kid got an offer for a deal from the prosecutor a while back he should've taken, but didn't. Now we're a few days away from trial, he's getting worried and is pissed he's too late to grab it."

"You need better clients."

"I know. We're working on it."

"Good, you ready to head out?"

"Yeah. Let me lock up."

She heads for her office, grabbing her purse. We've been back and settled in our respective offices for a few weeks now. We're both making a few adjustments to our schedules, and one of the perks is most days we're able to drive in together.

We did this morning with our bags already packed and in the back of my truck. We're driving straight to the airport to catch our flight for a long weekend with her parents. We weren't able to hold off visiting them any longer.

My guys will keep the office running while I'm gone, but Reagan closed hers because Sally is taking the dog this weekend.

We make it in record time, despite the rush hour.

"Do you have the tickets?" Reagan asks when we walk into

the terminal.

"All set."

I pat my chest pocket as I lead the way to security. I checked in online and we just packed a carry-on bag each, although I'm afraid Reagan may be pissed about that when she discovers we're not going to Phoenix as we planned.

There isn't much time to spare once we clear security to get to our gate. As I'd hoped, Reagan doesn't really question my lead and she doesn't bother checking the screen when the attendant rushes us on board.

It's not until we're seated in the business class seats I upgraded us to, sipping a drink, when the voice of the pilot over the intercom announces our destination, and Reagan clues in.

"We're on the wrong plane," she hisses, trying to get her seat belt unbuckled.

I cover her fumbling hands with one of mine to stop her.

"No, we're not."

Her head swings around, eyes shooting fire.

"We can't go to Vegas, Mom and Dad are waiting at the airport."

"They will be...in Vegas."

Now she looks confused. Even more so when I produce the ring I had burning a hole in my pocket since I took it out of the safe in my office.

"What are you doing?" she whispers.

"Your parents drove to Vegas yesterday. Jackson and Catherine and the girls arrived there this morning."

Her gorgeous eyes shimmer as the tears start pooling.

"Cal..."

"Next weekend we'll have a big party at your place, celebrating with our friends. Pooja and Sally have been working on that. But this weekend is just for us, with family." I swallow hard to keep my composure when the first tears start rolling down her flushed cheeks. "I should be down on one knee, but I might not be able to get back up."

"I don't care."

"I love you, Reagan. It was clear from the start, the woman I'd heard so much about over the years was all of those things and so much more. All it took was a few seconds in your presence to recognize how perfect you would be at my side. These past few months have shown how right I was." I lift her hand and slip the ring I bought weeks ago over the tip of her finger. "Make me the absolute luckiest bastard on the face of the earth and be my wife?"

She's now full-on smiling through her tears, nodding furiously.

"You're crazy, and presumptuous, and conniving, and I love you so much...so yes. Yes, I'd be honored."

I slide the ring down her finger and the next moment she has her belt undone, climbing on my lap without any regard for the curious glances we're drawing. I keep my eyes open on hers as she kisses me, the connection conveying everything for which there aren't words to describe.

"I'm so sorry." The soft, apologetic voice belongs to a flight attendant leaning over us. "We're about to take off. You really should buckle into your seat."

"Of course." Reagan scrambles back over the armrest and buckles in.

"Thanks," the woman smiles and adds, "and congratulations."

With the plane taxiing down the runway, Reagan grabs my hand, entwining our fingers.

"I can't believe you did this," she says, turning her head my way.

"Jumping in the deep end, Sweetheart. This was the only piece missing."

I reach over and cover the barely-there bump of her belly with my hand as we take off.

THE END

THE SALVATION SOCIETY

Thank you for reading, we hope you enjoyed this Salvation Society novel. Clink on the link below to become a member of the Society and and keep up with your beloved SEALs.

JOIN THE SOCIETY

https://www.subscribepage.com/SSsignup

Want to read more stories in The Salvation Society?
Click below for a complete list of titles:
https://www.thesalvationsociety.com/all-books/

ACKNOWLEDGMENTS

First and foremost I want to express my gratitude to *Corinne Michaels* for allowing me to play in her world and with her characters! I am beyond excited.

I would also like to thank *Crystal Ann* who has been so patient and professional, helping me navigate the details of this collaboration.

And of course, as always, I'm thankful for the amazing team of people without whom you would not be reading my books. They keep me on the straight and narrow.

I'm blessed with a fabulous editing/proofreading team, *Karen Hrdlicka* and *Joanne Thompson*, who have taught me all I need to know about the English language.

Perhaps less visible but equally important are; my agent, *Stephanie Phillips* of SBR Media; my publicists, *Debra Presley & Drue Hoffman* of Buoni Amici Press; and my personal assistant, *Krystal Weiss*.

To all the wonderful bloggers, who spread the word of every new release, I thank you for your time, your efforts, and your loyalty over the years.

And finally to all of you, my readers, THANK YOU. You

take a chance on me with every new book you open, and I can't thank you enough for putting your faith in me.

Love you all.

BOOKS BY FREYA BAKER

For all available books click HERE!
(https://books2read.com/ap/8YokmR/Freya-Barker)

STANDALONE BOOKS:

WHEN HOPE ENDS

VICTIM OF CIRCUMSTANCE

PASS SERIES:

HIT & RUN

LIFE&LIMB

ARROW'S EDGE SERIES:

EDGE OF REASON

EDGE OF DARKNESS

EDGE OF TOMORROW

(coming September 2020)

ON CALL SERIES (Operation Alpha):

BURNING FOR AUTUMN

COVERING OLLIE

TRACKING TAHLULA

ABSOLVING BLUE

REVEALING ANNIE

(coming August 2020)

ROCK POINT SERIES:

KEEPING 6

CABIN 12

HWY 550

10-CODE

NORTHERN LIGHTS COLLECTION:

A CHANGE IN TIDE

A CHANGE OF VIEW

A CHANGE OF PACE

SNAPSHOT SERIES:

SHUTTER SPEED

FREEZE FRAME

IDEAL IMAGE

PORTLAND, ME, NOVELS:

FROM DUST

CRUEL WATER

THROUGH FIRE

STILL AIR

LULLAY (A Christmas novella)

CEDAR TREE SERIES:

SLIM TO NONE

HUNDRED TO ONE

AGAINST ME

CLEAN LINES

UPPER HAND

LIKE ARROWS

HEAD START

ABOUT THE AUTHOR

USA Today bestselling author Freya Barker loves writing about ordinary people with extraordinary stories.

Driven to make her books about 'real' people; she creates characters who are perhaps less than perfect, each struggling to find their own slice of happy, but just as deserving of romance, thrills and chills in their lives.

Recipient of the ReadFREE.ly 2019 Best Book We've Read All Year Award for "Covering Ollie, the 2015 RomCon "Reader's Choice" Award for Best First Book, "Slim To None", and Finalist for the 2017 Kindle Book Award with "From Dust", Freya continues to add to her rapidly growing collection of published novels as she spins story after story with an endless supply of bruised and dented characters, vying for attention!

Freya
Website (https://www.freyabarker.com)
Facebook Page (https://www.facebook.com/FreyaBarkerWrites)
Reader Group (https://www.facebook.com/
groups/FreyasBarksandBites/)
Twitter (https://twitter.com/freya_barker)
BookBub (https://www.bookbub.com/authors/freya-barker)
Instagram (https://www.instagram.com/freyabarker.writes/)
Or sign up for my newsletter:
https://www.subscribepage.com/Freya_Newsletter